HAVING IT BOTH WAYS

SELF-SUBVERSION IN WESTERN POPULAR CLASSICS

HAVING IT BOTH WAYS

SELF-SUBVERSION IN WESTERN POPULAR CLASSICS

Forrest G. Robinson

UNIVERSITY OF NEW MEXICO PRESS
ALBUQUERQUE

Chapter 1 appeared as "Uncertain Borders: Race, Sex, and Civilization in *The Last of the Mohicans,*" *Arizona Quarterly* 47 (1991): 1–28; a version of chapter 2 has been published as "The Virginian and Molly in Paradise: How Sweet Is It?" *Western American Literature* 21 (1986): 27–38; chapter 3 came out as "The Eyes Have It: An Essay on Jack London's *The Sea-Wolf,*" *American Literary Realism* 18 (1985): 178–95; a shorter version of chapter 4 appeared as "Heroism, Home, and the Telling of *Shane,*" *Arizona Quarterly* 45 (1989): 72–100; and a briefer rendering of chapter 5 was published as "The New Historicism and the Old West," *Western American Literature* 25 (1990): 103–23.

© 1993 BY THE UNIVERSITY OF NEW MEXICO PRESS
All rights reserved.
First edition

Library of Congress Cataloging-in-Publication Data

Robinson, Forrest G. (Forrest Glen), 1940–
   Having it both ways: self-subversion in western popular classics/Forrest G. Robinson.—1st ed.
      p.   cm.
   Includes bibliographical references and index.
   ISBN 0-8263-1453-8
   1. Western stories—History and criticism. 2. Popular literature—West (U.S.)—History and criticism.
3. American fiction—History and criticism. 4. West (U.S.) in literature. 5. Self in literature. I. Title.
PS374.W4R6   1993   92-39359
813.009'3278—dc20   CIP

FOR RENATE (A.K.A. GROVER)

CONTENTS

ACKNOWLEDGMENTS IX

INTRODUCTION 1

1. THE LAST OF THE MOHICANS 13

2. THE VIRGINIAN 41

3. THE SEA-WOLF 55

4. SHANE 79

5. THEORETICAL POSTSCRIPT 111

NOTES 145

INDEX 157

*It seems to me that we are, at least on paper,
supposed to be different from, or better than, we are.
And that kind of irritation confronts us all the time
and has from the very beginning. The Constitution
was a precipitate of all the best Enlightenment
thinking of Europe, and it's really quite a remarkable
document. That we don't manage to live up to it
is the source of all our self-analysis.*

E. L. Doctorow
Essays and Conversations

ACKNOWLEDGMENTS

A number of friends and colleagues have offered very helpful commentary on parts of this book. I am most deeply indebted to Steve Tatum, whose careful reading of the entire manuscript and subsequent counsel on matters of detail have been invaluable. I have a large debt as well to Stephen Greenblatt, both for advice on specific questions and for his stimulating example as a student of cultural poetics. Jerome Frisk, a tireless, penetrating, sympathetic critic, has on several occasions helped me to find my way. Michael Cowan has somehow made time to read most of this; he has been a constant source of insight and support. Susan Gillman has been unfailingly generous with her time and critical savvy. I am also grateful for helpful responses from Paige Baty, Bill Bloodworth, Catherine Carlstroem, Brian Collins, Daniel Duane, John Dizikes, Annette Gordon, John Jordan, Ann Lane, Vivian Sobchack, and Hayden White. Finally, I have enjoyed the loving support of a wonderful family—my wife, Colleen, and my daughters Grace, Renate, Emma, and Marie. They make it all worthwhile.

INTRODUCTION

This is a study of American culture as it is manifest in some of our most popular books. Those that I study in closest detail—*Riders of the Purple Sage, The Last of the Mohicans, The Virginian, The Sea-Wolf,* and *Shane*—are all in some sense "Westerns," though the characteristic patterns they betray, like the large audiences they have enjoyed, are hardly regional in any narrow way. They are broadly American in their heroes, who are cut from cloth that has endured more than two centuries of heavy wear. The great popularity of these books is quite obviously the result of this emphasis on the heroic, with its abundance of vigorous action in colorful settings, and its attention to such values as courage, independence, self-reliance, and the stoical indifference to pain. We come back to these books, and we urge them on our children, because they tell this familiar and very gratifying story about ourselves.

I argue in what follows that they do much more than this. If these books reinforce our sense of the heroic, they also challenge it. If they dramatize the triumph of American virtues, they also explore the dark side of a dominant self-image. If they dwell on the exploits of white men, they are also peculiarly alive to the grave injustices of the social order they portray, especially as those injustices bear on people of color and women. But although all of these texts feature sharp contrasts in shading and emphasis, none appears to do so in a fully controlled or premeditated way. Each of the novels seems on its face to celebrate a leading article of the national faith, yet each betrays an impulse, a self-subversive reflex, to undermine what it appears so clearly to approve. James Fenimore Cooper is intermittently and rather obliquely in touch with the subversive undertow in his "history" of frontier heroism, but he is never the master of its pull on the surface of his narrative. Jack Schaefer, on the other hand, gives no evidence of glimpsing the penetrating critique of male hegemony that *Shane* so brilliantly performs. We are thus witness in these novels to the operations of a kind of textual unconscious, a subtle, generally unobserved, but nonetheless quite pronounced subversive resistance to conventional heroic perspectives.

In their characteristic tensions, their simultaneous thrust and counterthrust, the books assembled here present themselves as sites for the negotiation of competing perspectives on the issues of race and gender. As such, they are evidence of an enduring dialectic on questions of major cultural significance conducted, if much less frequently observed, in our popular discourse. This is no small claim. It runs directly contrary to the common assumption that popular culture achieves its broad currency by veering away from contested issues, or by raising them briefly, only in order to "manage" or "contain" them. Moreover, it involves the corollary that the audience engages actively with the text in the subtleties of negotiation. I advance an explanation for the fact that this collaboration between artifact and audience generally goes unnoticed, even by experts in the field.

These novels are enduringly popular, I argue, because they give us access to an ongoing cultural conversation on central, painfully vexing questions of power and authority. Again, this is not to suggest that my authors and their readers are fully attentive to the complexity of their own discourse. To the contrary, I have found that we enter this conversation almost without recognizing what we are doing. The popular text joins with its audience in having it both ways in areas where social practices depart painfully from leading public ideals. It is not a conspiracy of silence; nor is it a resolute evasion. Rather, popular texts approach and retreat from a contested center, and they enable a similar pattern of address and withdrawal in their readers. They operate through a variety of dodges and feints, displacements and tradeoffs, dimly concealed acknowledgments and dimly acknowledged concealments. They have endured, I argue, because they give us a window on major cultural embarrassments, *and* because they open it no more than half way. Indeed, we are compelled to return to

INTRODUCTION

these subtly mingled narratives precisely because we never see them fully through.

Popularity is thus the issue of an always incomplete negotiation and renegotiation of questions that we have neither fully resolved nor fully banished from sight and mind. The reader, I want to insist, is an active party to such partial resolutions, but so, in varying ways, are writers and the books they produce. It is a complex sort of collaboration that I have in mind—a subtle give and take whose precise terms and dynamics vary from one text to another. But the result is invariably an unstable compromise between assertions of prominent social and political ideals on one hand, and unsettling glimpses of lapses from those same ideals on the other. I define this contradictory, self-subversive tendency—this having things both ways—as *bad faith*, the reciprocal deception of self and other in the denial of departures from leading public values. I have reserved detailed discussion of the dynamics of this process for the Theoretical Postscript at the end of this volume. I do this because such general perspectives as I have to offer are the products of numerous local engagements, spread out over nearly a decade, with specific literary texts. Thus the theoretical position that I have arrived at is tentative and incomplete, a kind of report on work in progress. As such it appears—where I am persuaded it belongs—as the sequel to a sampling of the critical practice from which it has arisen.

Suffice it here to say that Western literary discourse, especially of the popular variety, betrays a persistent pattern of doubleness, or self-subversion, in which conflicting moral perspectives compete for preeminence. Or so I have found it. In a novel such as *Tom Sawyer*, for example, the analysis of the mechanisms by which people have it both ways may be said to fill the foreground. If we readers miss the point, it is probably because the villagers are so baldly and comically harmless in their duplicity that they pose no particular challenge to our equanimity. With *Huckleberry Finn*, on the other hand, the moral issue is so graphic and so painful that combined and rather frantic maneuverings by Mark Twain, by Huck, and by the reader alike yield only the shakiest of evasions.[1] In other novels, pressing moral issues are addressed, only to get lost in what may strike us, upon reflection, as telling flights to confusion. Zane Grey's fabulously popular *Riders of the Purple Sage* retreats in just this way behind a kind of smoke screen. It was one of Grey's "rules for . . . literary work" that "in everything there is always something undiscovered." The writer's task, he believed, was to "find it."[2] One senses that Grey was himself groping for the "undiscovered" in *Riders of the Purple Sage,* that he was trying to make sense of the baffling portents that arose at his touch from such subjects as love, sex, violence, and the nexus of civilization, progress, and evolution. There can be little doubt that Grey had a hankering to address the leading social issues of his time. He was concerned, most clearly, about conflicting conceptions of male and female identity. But he was at the same time unwilling to confront the full implications of his own insights on such questions. What is truth? he asked, and would not stay for an answer.

It is one thing to be confused, another to be deliberately evasive. It is a species of bad faith, I suppose, to conceal one's confusion—however unconscious that confusion may be—in a novel that makes an implicit claim to coherence. But, then, *Riders of the Purple Sage* is not, as Grey well knew, a novel. It is a romance, which—by contrast with the novel—makes no pretense to realism or verisimilitude. Almost by definition, the romance—and especially the popular Western romance—has things both ways. As Wayne Ude argues, the "romance-adventure-novel" as practiced by the likes of Grey generally arrives at "morally correct"—if "limited and shallow"—conclusions by way of baffling twists and mystifications.[3] To the extent, then, that the book's confusion is at once indulged and to some extent concealed, the bad faith inheres in the form of the fiction, in the genre of romance-adventure, and in the license that goes with it.

An example. As a romancer Grey need not apologize for waiting until the end of his narrative to reveal that Jane Withersteen's resistance to Lassiter is grounded not merely in high religious and moral scruple—she insists time and again that he must learn to love his enemies—but also in the shameful knowledge that her father was deeply complicit in the wrongdoing that Lassiter seeks to revenge. She is in bad faith in keeping that knowledge from him, in concealing her personally interested motive in a righteous one. But is Grey equally remiss in keeping this detail from us? If, as I am inclined to believe, Grey's characterization of Jane is at one level an attempt to address the contemporary "woman question," then the answer is yes. For even as it helps to explain Jane's otherwise rather inexplicable opposition to the gunman's feud with the Mormon leadership, the belated revelation of her secret shame undermines her earlier, anguished resistance on the grounds of religious scruple, and at the same time compounds the confusion that attaches to the pronounced erotic strain in her motivation. Thus the new information renders Jane's position more plausible, but morally less defensible; she seems more real, perhaps, but less ideal.

Less ideal, I would add, than Grey intended. He had it in mind, I believe, to represent Jane as a woman of great religious faith and moral fiber who is misled by unscrupulous hypocrites but brought round by a good, strong man to a proper compromise between religious conviction and realistic necessity. *Riders of the Purple Sage*, as Jane Tompkins observes, was engaged in a kind of dialogue with the "domestic" fiction of its era—with novels in which women take the lead in advocating a host of "feminine" virtues, among them peace and Christian love. Tompkins takes the view that authors like Owen Wister and Zane Grey were writing in direct reaction to such books. The popular Western, she argues, "owes its essential character to the dominance of a women's culture in the nineteenth century and to women's invasion of the public sphere between 1880 and 1920." There can be little quarrel with the notion that books like *Riders of the Purple Sage* were sites for the negotiation of competing male and female agendas. But it is quite another thing to claim, as Tompkins does, that the Western flatly rejected the values embodied in the domestic fiction of the period. *Riders of the Purple Sage* "insists," she says, "that you can't live by Christian love because if you do you'll be destroyed. The truth the novel asserts is that Jane Withersteen's goodness and mercy . . . and the whole Judeo-Christian tradition it represents won't work when the chips are down."[4]

But Grey was not nearly this clear and unequivocal in his thinking on such matters. To claim, as Tompkins does, that *Riders of the Purple Sage* is the polar "antithesis of the cult of domesticity" is to credit Grey with greater lucidity than he possessed.[5] He does not simply align women with peaceful Christian charity on one side, against violent, godless men on the other. Consider that Venters has wearied utterly of his solitary ways, and longs "for the sound of a voice, the touch of a hand"[6]—for a wife and home at a safe remove from the violence of the West. Recall too that Lassiter warms to Jane's position on forgiveness, acknowledges respectfully that where he "was raised a woman's word was law"—adding, "I ain't quite outgrowed that yet" (101)—and takes flight to Surprise Canyon precisely that he may exchange his guns for a version of domestic life. It was Grey himself, after all, who insisted that "love . . . is only another name for romance," and that his own romances were written to prove "that hard men of the open also climb to the heights of nobility and sacrifice, to a supreme proof of the evolution of man, to a realization of God."[7] True enough, he stumbles in his fundamentally sympathetic characterization of Jane, who verges at points toward self-delusion. But her problems—her having things both ways—are more deeply grounded in sex and pride than in religion. Her maker's attitude toward "women's" values, meanwhile, though demonstrably mingled and even contradictory, was hardly hostile. Of course Grey might well have responded that in demanding consistency and coherence of his story we are simply barking up the wrong generic tree. To which we might reply that he favored the romance form because of its manifest tolerance for the kinds of confusion that he was prone to. In Grey's case, at least—as opposed, say, to Hawthorne's—the choice of genre was itself symptomatic of a penchant for having things both ways.

In fairness to Grey, let us try another tack, and allow—as he seems at points to want us to allow—that *Riders of the Purple Sage* is itself a fictional survey of just the sorts of deception that I have been describing. At the extreme we have the male leaders of the Mormon church, heartless hypocrites whose zeal is transparently a cover for ruthless lust and greed. They have it both ways, to be sure, though it is hardly clear that they are self-deceived in the matter. Tull and Dyer's dogmatism and hypocrisy are not so much the occasion for moral and psychological analysis as a foil for the greater virtue of Lassiter and Jane, Venters and Bess. Where the elders are fixed in their evil ways, the younger heroic protagonists are all earnest searchers after truth and justice; they aspire to goodness, and they display no little potential for positive change. Bess is the most mysterious. Nameless, virtually without an identity (or a fixed gender), effortlessly possessed, she emerges under Venters' guidance into love and self-respect. It is tellingly a feature of her blankness, her profound anonymity, that she is "innocent."

Venters is a more complete human being, yet it is hard to know what precisely to make of the developments in his character. He is initially a man out of love with solitude, yet notably slow—stupidly slow, in fact—to recognize that he is in love with Bess. The real obstacle here, which he never seems to acknowledge and perhaps never consciously grasps, is his jealous suspicion that Bess is not a virgin. Grey's bad faith on this score—his evident if unacknowledged adherence to a double standard—registers in the furtive resort to innuendo and euphemism. Even as Venters ponders whether Bess is the product of "a tragic fate rather than a natural leaning to evil" (80), we feel the pressure of his own desire, his own repressed "leaning to evil," to take what he would condemn the girl for giving, or even for having taken from her. He decides early on that she is "innocent," but that judgment is quite evidently the function of an unutterable wish. Indeed, so durable is Venters's sexual jealousy of Oldring that it provokes him to murder the suspected offender. This is a messy business, not least because it appears that Oldring is Bess's father. The deep flaw in Grey's sexual scheme of things surfaces abruptly and tragically in Venters's fatal error. Yet the grave social implication of the deed is at least partially evaded when it is discovered that Bess is in fact the daughter of Frank Erne. This gets Venters off the hook, and saves the match, but at a heavy strain on our credulity. Romance again.

In Venters's characterization we are witness to Grey's bad faith retreat from the implications of complex social issues—the sexual double standard, male violence—that apparently troubled him, but that he lacked the wherewithal to resolve. In the upshot, he had it both ways. Bess is acceptable to Venters on any terms, but of course she is not. Vengeance, we are told, is "utterly foreign to [Venters's] nature" (200), yet "his passion to kill" prevails, and he lets blood with relish, and with Grey's apparent approval. All of this in the name of love—and yet a love that is conditional on an "innocence" over which Bess has virtually no control, and which expresses itself in gestures of outright possession ("She belongs to me!" [109]). Most puzzling of all, perhaps, Venters fully acknowledges his love for Bess only when she discovers a fortune in gold in their remote hideaway. "I love you! I'm free!" he exults; "I'm a man—a man you've made—no more a beggar!" (194). Venters first tastes the "unutterable sweetness of desire" (158) in Surprise Valley, but there is far more of social significance in his discovery than he, or Grey, can finally manage. Again, the romance form serves as a kind of safety valve when the pressure of implication gets too high.

We are prepared, I suppose, to accept the idea that love and vengeance may at times go hand in hand. We are no doubt just as willing

INTRODUCTION

to entertain the notion that true love knows nothing of violence. *Riders of the Purple Sage* asks us to accept both of these ideas, and to do so, apparently, without trying to find a way between them. Certainly the narrative has it both ways on this score. Jane has "one absolute and unfaltering hold on ultimate and supreme justice. That was love. 'Love your enemies as yourself!' was a divine word, entirely free from any church or creed" (176). So firm and persuasive is her position that she actually brings Lassiter to give up his guns. "Come with me out of Utah," he pleads (in a manner that would make the Virginian blush for shame), so "I can put away my guns an' be a man." But even as Lassiter surrenders the symbols of his manhood, Jane returns them. "With blundering fingers" she "buckled the belt round his waist where it belonged" (226–27). As if to further compound the confusion, Grey subsequently brings Lassiter back to his vengeful self and restores Jane to her elevated Christian principles. But neither is finally any surer than Grey is—or, perhaps, than we are—about the "correct" place to stand. Little wonder that they run away to a secret canyon and lock the door. Life is much too complicated. *"Don't—look—back!"* (246) Lassiter cries as they gallop out of Mormon country, leaving the past, and all of its dizzying moral dilemmas, behind.

This is of course to oversimplify. As William Bloodworth and others have clearly shown, the motivation of the leading actors in *Riders of the Purple Sage* is deeply, if everywhere obliquely, sexual in origin. Grey's "characters often experience intense internal conflict," Bloodworth observes. "And often in a more complicated and subtle way than we might expect, the conflict comes down to sexual desire."[8] Lassiter is more self-aware than the others in this regard. "I'm burnin' up with hell's fire," he admits. Jane is less well attuned to the reality of her feelings. "Oh, Lassiter," she replies reproachfully, "no—no—you don't love me that way!" (131), even though her treatment—or better, perhaps, her *management*—of the cowboy has from the beginning been premised on just the opposite assumption. For all of her agonizing about Christian love, Jane is most adroit, if also conspicuously self-deceived, in her sexual maneuvering.[9] To a point, Grey controls this dimension of the story. Jane is at one point compared to Delilah (226); at another she concedes that she has "made love" to Lassiter in order "to bind his hands" (128). But she persists in the belief, as Grey seems to, that the Christian preservation of life and

INTRODUCTION

peace is her sole objective, and that there is little of the erotic in what moves her.

Yet in this, as the text makes abundantly clear, Jane and her maker are wildly deluded. Jane's fascination with Lassiter's guns is only the most obvious of numerous indications that her rage to control the cowboy is sexually driven. Submerged in the resolute Christian peacemaker is the stereotypical emasculator. Thus in laboring to portray a fundamentally good—intelligent, independent, generous, upright—woman, Grey inadvertently betrays his own deepest fears about the opposite sex. One might develop this point in considerable detail. But in fact the emergent critical consensus is already clear. Grey's repressed fascination with sexuality—and especially with feminine sexuality—expressed itself, as William Bloodworth argues, in a doubling pattern of "arousal" and "recontainment," of glancing, largely unconscious revelations operating in tandem with dutiful concealments of what has been revealed. It was a matter, simply, of having it both ways—for Grey himself, for characters like Venters and Jane, and for morally fastidious readers who secretly crave a little spice in their literary diet.[10]

But the price to be paid for having things both ways is confusion, contradiction, bafflement. Grey dealt with this problem, as I have already suggested, by retreating to the permitting conventions of romance. Readers by the millions have dealt with it, presumably, by adopting a version of T. K. Whipple's first rule for reading Zane Grey: "We must never ask of him truth to the actual world as we know it."[11] There has been more to the audience response than this, I would argue, though a widespread loosening of "realistic" expectations is undoubtedly an element in Grey's popularity. In fact, *Riders of the Purple Sage* addresses itself to leading social issues, but it does so without enforcing focused deliberation or a movement toward closure. As the return on their indulgence of the book's confusion, readers are permitted to have things both ways, to see and turn away, to approach matters of genuine concern, but without sustained challenges to their prepossessions. The "actual world" is thus not so much avoided as negotiated, brought to terms.

The dynamics of reader response to *Riders of the Purple Sage* are clearly prefigured in the way Grey's major characters deal with the baffling surfaces of their world. They are all confronted with major questions about identity and sexuality, and to a point they are all willing to entertain alternatives to their leading assumptions. But that point is quickly reached. Venters is regularly overcome with the sense that the world and his feelings about it are ungraspable—"unreal" (98), as he puts it to himself. Still, he acquiesces readily enough in the confusion. After all, he decides, "to dream is happiness," while thinking "clearly" is not. Hence his delight in Surprise Canyon, where he finds contentment "living a beautiful dream." "How glorious it would be," he muses, to stay in his remote hideaway, "and never think again" (160–61). Bess has a similar aversion to sustained reflection. "I'm happy when I don't think," she tells Venters, and settles into mindless action as a cure for what ails her (152–53).

Meanwhile, as her entanglements grow more complex and compromising, Jane observes that "she had lost, or had never gained, the whole control of her mind. In some measure reason and wisdom and decision were locked in a chamber of her brain, awaiting a key. Power to think of some things was taken from her" (169). As her settled response to a confusing reality, Jane agreed with Lassiter that "things aren't what they seem." They decide that there is a measure of duplicity in all adult experience; thus in their own "falseness" they are "like the rest of the women, an' men, too." Jane insists that some of the "blinding scales" have fallen from her eyes. "But when I attempt serious thought I'm dazed," she goes on to admit. "I don't think. I don't care any more" (225). This is the mood the lovers take with them to Surprise Canyon. But the decision to fly from confusion is only apparently a spontaneous one. Jane's horses, the fastest in the territory, have been saddled and ready to ride from page one.

It is the key to Jane's bad faith, and to Venters' as well, that their incapacity for reflection repays them with blindness to what they prefer not to know about themselves. They secretly embrace confusion. It is of course the clear implication of their retreat from reflection that they have glimpsed the truth of things, and thought better of owning it. It is the same with readers who rush to forgive Grey his departures from verisimilitude; they too have an investment in blindness. Just so the novelist himself, who shrank from a full, conscious engagement with the contemporary social issues that caught his attention.

Grey professed to love the remote outdoors because in its solitude he felt within himself the resurgence of "the savage past." It was like being a boy again, "when like all boys" he "killed for the sake of killing, until conscience intervened." Conscience was "the difference between savage and civilized man," he argued; it was "the great factor in human progress." But it was not for all that an unmingled good in his estimation. Moral reflection was evidently a heavy blessing for Grey. He much preferred the oblivion—which he associated with savages and boys—that overtook him in the open spaces. "Thoughts do not oppress here," he wrote. Especially thoughts about his writing, which, not surprisingly, were conflicted and painful for him. "My state" in the great out-of-doors, he observed gratefully, "is one of languor, comfort, and dreaminess. It comes to me here—what I should most heed—the very things that are here. These can never fail me. Their meaning is the secret of life. Sweet rest and dreamful ease!"[12]

1

THE LAST OF THE MOHICANS

1

Michael Rogin has recently reminded us of the central—and highly vexed—place of the Indian in the American consciousness during the Age of Jackson. This was above all else a period of headlong westward expansion, involving wars and treaties that resulted in the brutal dispossession of the original dwellers on the land. "Indians had not mattered so much," Rogin observes, "since the colonial settlements. They would never matter so much again." We need to be reminded of the preeminent national concern with Indians during this period because historians "have failed," Rogin charges, "to place Indians at the center of Jackson's life. They have interpreted the Age of Jackson from every perspective but Indian destruction, the one from which it actually developed historically." This is so, Rogin clearly implies, because historians of the period have fallen heir to a legacy of bad faith rooted squarely in Jackson's Indian policy.[1]

Because white men, led by Jackson, could find no tolerable "moral resolution" to their cruel and lawless treatment of the indigenous peoples, they developed in its place, even as they seized the land and decimated its occupants, "a powerful, legitimating cultural myth." Civilization, they argued, must in the nature of things displace Indian savagery. Toward that benign providential end, it was the duty of the white "fathers," following the archpatriarch, Jackson himself—who insisted that Indian leaders refer to him as their "father"—to take a firm hand in guiding their Indian "children" along the path destiny had set before them. By virtue of this pious cultural hoax, Rogin ar-

CHAPTER 1

gues, predatory whites, hungry for land but restrained in principle by their own laws and Christian values, had things both ways. The irony of the situation was doubly cruel. "America had begun with a radical assertion of the power of men to control their fate," Rogin asserts "But the country progressed through the destruction of another set of men, and responsibility for that destruction could not be faced." Instead, the white fathers assigned responsibility for their actions to the resistless unfolding of God's plan. They took what they wanted, and contrived, by casting themselves as benevolent parents struggling in vain with ungrateful children—"dying Indians betrayed whites," went the complaint—to submerge their guilt. It was perfect bad faith, a mass collaboration, orchestrated from the top, to deny that leading articles of the national faith had been violated.[2]

The great popularity of James Fenimore Cooper's *The Last of the Mohicans* argues quite emphatically in support of Rogin's position. Indian wars figured prominently in the national self-image at the time that Cooper first acted on the impulse to become a writer. By the mid-1820s, when he conceived and wrote his best seller, major developments in Federal Indian Removal Policy were regularly in the public eye. There can be no doubt that Cooper was keenly aware of these ominous signs. The title and dominant thematics of *The Last of the Mohicans* are the surest kind of evidence that he was alert and responsive to the gathering swell of legislation and public opinion that would sweep the Indians from their homes. At no time since its publication in 1826 has the novel's subtitle, *A Narrative of 1757*, served to diminish any informed reader's awareness of its direct relevance to contemporary affairs.

The popularity of the *The Last of the Mohicans* is also evidence that Cooper's representation of Indian-white relations won the approval of the American reading public. This was no mean feat. For his story of violent racial conflict, dispossession, and annihilation amounted to an indictment, at times direct, at others oblique, of the young Republic that was rapidly spreading across the continent. As George Sand quite astutely observed, "Cooper was able, without too great an affront to the pride of his country, to plead the cause of the Indians." He succeeded in this unlikely project, Sand suggests, because his novel was the occasion for a purgative expression of grief and guilt. In "the calm but resonant voice of the novelist," she argues, "the American let loose from his breast this conscience-stricken cry: 'In order to be what we are, we had to kill a great people and devastate a mighty land'"[3]

In the century and more since Sand composed these views, there has been ample confirmation of her basic insights. Modern critics regularly observe that *The Last of the Mohicans* addressed itself to what was, and what continues to be, an extremely sensitive question: How are we to square our sense of ourselves as a just and compassionate people with the cruelty and injustice that surface everywhere in the record of our dealings with the Indians? In Cooper's time, as I have indicated, the leading justification for the seizure of Indian land was the alleged moral superiority of Christian civilization to the "barbarism" of the displaced natives. Contact with Europeans, it was argued, worked to the Indians' moral and spiritual advantage. Cooper himself adopts this position in *Notions of the Americans* (1828), observing of Indian removal: "A great, humane, and, I think, rational project, is now in operation to bring the Indians within the pale of civilization."[4] But *Notions*—"a book written," as James Franklin Beard observes, "primarily for European readers"[5]—is notorious for its defensive idealization of the state of the nation. It is also laced with observations that run directly counter to Cooper's optimism. He notes, for example, that Indians are prone to "become victims to the abuses of civilization, without ever attainting to any of its moral elevation." Even more ominously, he reflects on Indian removal that "where there is much intercourse between the very strong and the very weak, there is always a tendency in the human mind to suspect abuses of power."[6] Certainly it is this latter, much darker perspective that dominates in *The Last of the Mohicans*. The novel is drenched in the blood that flows from the abuses of civilization and its power.

In fact, modern critics have gone a long step or two further than George Sand, both in stressing the novel's challenge to leading contemporary assumptions about Indian-white relations and in their attempts to reconcile its great popularity with this marked subversive thrust. More perhaps than any other Leatherstocking tale, *The Last of the Mohicans* brings the reader face to face with, in the words of Richard Drinnon, "the westward course of empire as a moral problem: How could a system of justice in the clearings be built upon a record of injustice in the wilderness? A society of Christian brotherhood erected upon its denial? Respect for law and order based on broken treaties, bribery and debauchery, and a thoroughgoing contempt for the natural rights of natives?"[7] Under the circumstances, Drinnon replies, these noble goals could not be achieved; the contradictions were too numerous and too massive. Kindred judgments might well result from a reading of *The Last of the Mohicans*. It is a story, after all, whose hero insists that racial hatred and revenge are "unsuitable to my colour and my religion," but who indulges both; who advises Duncan Heyward that "to outwit the knaves it is lawful to practise things, that may not be naturally the gift of a white skin"; and who, in the heat of battle, shouts, "Exterminate the varlets! no quarter to an accursed Mingo!"[8] And yet for most readers, the novel has not seemed to enforce Drinnon's grave conclusions. Contemporary American reviewers faulted Cooper for a variety of artistic shortcomings, but rarely if ever for the moral consistency of his tale.[9] Over the years the novel has enjoyed a reputation as a classic of frontier adventure, quite suitable for children, not as a fictional treatment of our culture's pathologies.

It is hardly my intention to quarrel with the views of critics who, like Drinnon, have found in *The Last of the Mohicans* a representation and emergent analysis of the racial tensions and habits of violence that have plagued our history and culture. The novel is conspicuously the product of its era in its address to the question, posed most directly by Michael Rogin, "How reconcile the destruction of the Indians with the American self-image?"[10] But I do want to look more closely at the fact that "this conscience-stricken cry" has enjoyed a large, enduring, and equable—not to say morally complacent—American popular audience. It is as though the vast majority of the novel's readers have somehow failed to recognize the clear drift of the narrative. How has this happened?

Other scholars have already given their more or less direct attention to this question. Michael Rogin's analysis is valuable in a general way because it reveals, relentlessly but persuasively, the ways in which Jackson and his contemporaries evaded the manifest immorality of their treatment of the Indians. Americans were aware of the chasm that separated their professed commitments to justice and Christian benevolence from the painful realities of the situation, but that awareness and those realities registered most frequently in assorted rationalizations and disclaimers. In Jackson's case, "the more egregious the activity, the more he engaged in falsification of memory, denial, militant self-righteousness, and projection of his own motivations onto others." More generally, Americans were encouraged to regard "Indian destruction as an abstracted and generalized process removed from human control and human reality."[11] According to Richard Drinnon, Thomas Jefferson was equally at pains to hide "from himself and others the meaning of Indian extermination." Toward this end, he had at his disposal "two time-tested" strategies of evasion: he could claim that the "childish Indians were especially prone to manipulation by tyrannous outside forces," or he could insist that "Indian savages were especially merciless."[12] Such historical perspectives are useful because they illustrate that there was widespread public concern with "the Indian problem" in Cooper's time, and because they suggest that such concern most often expressed itself in resistance to the truth. Not surprisingly, several of the most familiar varieties of denial turn up in *The Last of the Mohicans*. We are at numerous points in the narrative reminded that the removal and destruction of the Indians is a manifestation of America's destiny. It is clear from the outset that "the cold and selfish policy of the distant monarchs of Europe" (11) is at the bottom of the trouble in the wilderness, and examples of Indian cruelty are everywhere in evidence—most conspicuously, of course, in the terrible massacre at Fort William Henry.

I will have much more to say about the novel's evasions and their role in its great popularity. First, however, let me broach a related question that bears on every text discussed in this book, but that I will deal with fully only in my concluding chapter. If it is true, as I will argue again and again, that the denial of painful moral and social implications is a key to the wide appeal of some of our favorite books, then why, we may wonder, do these books feature such awkward elements in the first place? Why not simply and completely exclude such painful materials and thereby eliminate the evasions they give rise to? Or, to put it another way, why would a fledgling novelist such as James Fenimore Cooper, ambitious for popularity and attempting to rebound from the "unqualified failure" of *Lionel Lincoln*,[13] turn to a subject guaranteed to stir moral uneasiness and resistance in his audience? The question assumes, of course, that Cooper and his audience were fully conscious of the dynamics of their address to such matters. But the question also serves to underline the fact that

CHAPTER 1

the popular success of *The Last of the Mohicans* is somehow geared to its denial of what it at the same time painfully suggests about "the Indian problem."

We may begin to unravel this literary conundrum by turning to critics who give special emphasis to the observation, first ventured by George Sand, that Cooper and his readers were driven by the need to express their guilt about America's mistreatment of the Indians. Leslie Fiedler pursues this line of thought, insisting that in *The Last of the Mohicans*, "Cooper tells precisely the same sort of truth about the Indian that Mrs. Stowe was to tell about the negro: in each it is guilt that speaks, the guilt of a whole community."[14] John P. McWilliams echoes this position in his observation that "the barbarous greed of many of Cooper's white frontiersmen, and the eloquence of many a wronged but noble savage, argue that Cooper and many of his readers felt a need to expiate white guilt."[15] But the earliest and fullest modern version of this position is surely Roy Harvey Pearce's, as it unfolds in his very influential *Savages of America*. It is integral to Pearce's thesis that during Cooper's time and since, "writers of fiction" and their readers persuaded themselves

> that the Indian might well have been a noble savage but that his nobility, inferior to civilized nobility, could not survive the pressures of civilization. Their task came to be to put this truth down imaginatively, at once publicly to admit that the Indian had been cruelly destroyed and to satisfy themselves and their readers that that destruction was part of a universal moral progress which it was the special destiny of America to manifest. The myriad Indian fictions after 1823 are so many attempts to expiate the sin rising from the cruelty which was a necessary quality of American progress westward.

When it came to broken treaties, the provocation of one-sided wars, removal, and what amounted at times to outright genocide, Americans succeeded against great odds "in convincing themselves that they were right, divinely right. Only with such conviction—cruel, illogical, and self-indulgent as it was—could they move on." At the very foundation of this broad and continuing cultural exercise in denial are the Leatherstocking tales, in which "the idea of savagism is realized in the image of an Indian in his gifts at once noble and ignoble, an Indian whose fate it was to be a means of understanding a civilization in which he, by civilized definition, could not participate."[16]

In a number of perfectly obvious ways, not least in observing that the cruelty of the situation had, in some measure, to be represented before it could be rationalized, Pearce's commentary applies directly and quite usefully to *The Last of the Mohicans*. His remarks are also valuable as points of departure for a more detailed analysis of the novel's specific dynamics. For example, "to expiate" is not quite faithful to the thrust of Cooper's narrative, and, for that matter, to the much larger historical and cultural setting in which Pearce frames it. If by "to expiate" we mean to atone, then the verb fails to catch the all-important element of denial in both text and context. It is one thing to make amends, but quite another to ignore or deny the offense. And if an expiation is understood as a conscious act, then the term also misses the decidedly subliminal cast of the denials that Cooper, his novel, and his audience are engaged in.

But if it is an attempt to evade, and not to expiate, that we behold in Cooper and his culture, then clearly enough, that attempt fails. For while the novel has been popularly received as a romantic adventure, it is also quite conspicuously a long look at one of the most vexing moral issues of its day. *The Last of the Mohicans* undoubtedly reinforced the conviction that Americans were "right, divinely right," in their treatment of Indians, but it also serves quite well to support the opposite view. This is, I recognize, to repeat what I have already said. But it is to do so in a way that gives special emphasis to the simultaneity in the novel of the impulses to tell and to untell the same story. *The Last of the Mohicans* manages somehow to express guilt and to repress it at the same time; its readers may at one sitting feel the sting of conscience and the supportive hand of destiny in their response to the same, central issue. When it comes to "the Indian problem," in other words, the novel and its audience have it both ways.

2

The economy of denial in *The Last of the Mohicans* operates through a variety of means to represent, and to argue away, the terrible injustice that Americans recognized, but could not acknowledge directly or for long, in their treatment of the Indians. Most obviously, perhaps, in announcing itself as a history of warfare between Indians and Europeans, the novel neutralizes in some degree the sense of painful immediacy that its action would have stirred in contemporary readers. There is a similar distancing in the deaths of Cora and Uncas, and in the concluding slaughter of Hurons by Delawares, developments that portray the "palefaces" as victims and the Indians as bloody-minded aggressors against whites and other Indians alike. Such "unerring evidences of the ruthless results which attend an Indian vengeance" (339) are reminiscent of the terrible Indian massacre of unarmed British soldiers and their families at Fort William Henry. In describing this famous atrocity, argues James Franklin Beard, it was "Cooper's task . . . to invent an infrastructure to make the outrage dramatically intelligible and humanly meaningful."[17] For contemporary readers, the vividly graphic account of savage Indian violence must have served, in an indirect and unacknowledged sort of way, as "justification" for the behavior of such prominent leaders as Andrew Jackson. Casting Montcalm as the perfidious, if passive, accomplice to the slaughter and the English (with whom Cooper and his readers would have most closely identified) as helpless victims undoubtedly worked to reinforce this ensanguined if also strangely comforting portrait of long-suffering innocence.

But it is central to my understanding of *The Last of the Mohicans* that its gestures toward vindication are generally found in tension with countering gestures toward condemnation. The cry of innocence is in dialogue with an admission of guilt. If the Indians are brutal, treacherous, and cruel, so are their white adversaries. It is also perfectly clear that the British and their colonial allies come to grief because they are outnumbered, outflanked, outwitted, and subject to gross lapses of judgment. Such shortcomings are most manifest in Munro and Heyward, but they are present as well in the portrait of garrulous, often impulsive Hawk-eye, whose failures of tact and sensitivity contrast sharply with the delicacy of feeling and judgment displayed by his "savage" companions. Thus while the cause of civilization is at times the object of sympathy in *The Last of the Mohicans*, it is rarely if ever represented as worthy of real respect.

European pretensions to moral superiority are everywhere at large, and at issue, in the behavior of the story's putative hero, Natty Bumppo. Though he is often, and with some justice, characterized as a figure of "the middle ground" between the worlds of the Indian and the white, Natty is also the novel's most vigorous spokesman for civilized values. His insistence that he is pure white, with "no cross in his blood" (35), is quite explicitly an assertion of moral and spiritual preeminence. But Natty's compulsive reiteration of this claim is only the most obvious evidence that he is protesting too much. For all his advocacy of Christian principles, he is at least as predatory and quite as vengeful as the Indians he so habitually condemns. There is not, he brags, "the space of a square mile atwixt Horican and the river, that 'kill-deer' hasn't dropped a living body on, be it an enemy, or be it a brute beast" (136). He insists that "revenge is an Indian feeling, and all who know me, know that there is no cross in my veins"; but in the same breath he vows—"so long as flint will fire, or powder burn"—to get even with the "Frenchers" (183). The same, perfectly bald contradiction surfaces again a few pages later, when Natty announces: "Now, for myself, I do love justice; and therefore—I will not say I hate a Mingo, for that may be unsuitable to my colour and my religion—though I will just repeat, it may have been owing to the night that 'kill-deer' had no hand in the death of this skulking Oneida" (197). At the root of the problem, of course, is the utter incompatability of Christian morality with imperial warfare against Indians. Natty concedes this point in allowing that Christianity "is what I would wish to practyse myself, as one without a cross of blood, though it is not always easy to deal with an Indian, as you would with a fellow christian" (274). But the concession draws attention to, and hardly mitigates, the grave contradiction between his professions and his deeds.

The point to be emphasized here is that *The Last of the Mohicans* offers no clear, unequivocal perspective on "the Indian problem." Rather, the novel moves back and forth between what may be construed as defenses and indictments of the claims of civilization. Natty is at times perfectly plausible as a hero; but the negative weight of his example cannot have been lost entirely on his earliest readers. The scout wavers—and not merely in his morality, but in his theology as well. He runs rather fast and loose with the idea of Providence, and his notions about Heaven vary quite dramatically, depending—it seems clear—on his own stake in developments beyond the grave.[18] But Natty is hardly unique in his contradictory ways. *The Last of the Mohicans* is more generally remarkable for its tendency to subvert conventional distinctions and boundaries, especially as they bear on assumptions about the savage and the civilized. As I have noted previously, the conventional, morally comforting opposition of good palefaces and bad redskins is sometimes advanced in the novel, but it is also frequently undermined. The Indians are twice condemned ("thorough savages" [119]) for making a "revolting meal" (100) of raw meat, but Natty refers proudly to "stout detachments" of the Royal Americans who are "glad to eat their venison raw" (54). Savagery and vengefulness are hardly unique to the Indians, and there are no paternal and filial sentiments more tender than those exchanged between Chingachgook and Uncas (199–200).

Such breakdowns, it might be argued, are at the cutting edge of a conscious program for the exposure of the hollowness, and even the hypocrisy, of white moral pretensions. This view would be more defensible if it were not for the dramatic increase in boundary confusion that overtakes the action in the second half of the novel. Animals are taken for humans, humans pass for animals, disguises open borders between warring enemies, and perfect sanity is confused with feeble-mindedness in a sweeping collapse of rudimentary distinctions. Cooper's point in all this, according to Jane Tompkins, is to illustrate the "confusion of mutually exclusive systems of classification, which . . . occurs when disparate cultures collide with one another," and thus to impress upon the reader the absolute necessity of maintaining "the Anglo-Saxon tradition of racial purity." Cooper reinforces the same lesson in the massacre at Fort William Henry, where he "deliberately emphasizes the breakdown of all social controls," and in "Natty Bumppo's almost fanatical assertion throughout the novel that he is 'a man without a cross,' by which he means that he is of unmixed blood, pure stock."[19]

Tompkins's conception of Cooper contrasts quite sharply with the more common view that he was in some considerable degree out of conscious control of his materials. "There exists at the very heart of the book," argues Wayne Franklin, "a vision of chaos so profoundly upsetting that hardly anything remains untransformed by it." The artist's imaginative surrender to disorder makes fullest sense, he goes on, in the light of Susan Cooper's recollection that *The Last of the Mohicans* first arose in her father's mind during an attack of sunstroke: "We are left with the fact that the novel seems to have been dreamed as much as composed."[20] Thomas Philbrick is equally impressed with

Susan Cooper's startling revelation, and quite as inclined to argue that *The Last of the Mohicans* gives expression to unresolved contradictions emerging directly from the interior of "the dreamer and his dream." The novel, he suggests, is quite unlike anything else that Cooper wrote: "Its gestures toward historicity and toward novelistic convention are gestures merely, for here the ordering and informing intelligence of the artist succeeds in establishing only the most superficial control over the activities of the imagination."[21]

At one extreme, then, we have Cooper the mathematically precise social allegorist who deploys images of disorder in the service of a perfectly coherent sociological thesis;[22] at the other we have the artist-as-dreamer, the unreflecting purveyor of violent and chaotic unconscious promptings. There is, I believe, a large measure of truth in both of these views, but a measure of distortion as well. The latter position speaks usefully to the sense, shared by many readers, of the novel's headlong, accelerating pace, its excesses of violence, its numerous contradictions, and its fascination with disorder—its tone of strained resistance to the oneiric, the anomic, the repressed. "The incidents are too crowded," complained one early reviewer. "There are too many imminent dangers and hair-breadth escapes; far too much of the same sort of excitement; too many startling sights, and unearthly sounds, and amazing incidents."[23] This sense of the novel's perilous veering toward chaos is missing from Tompkins's account, in which the disorder is brought neatly into alignment with what she describes as "the requirements of an abstract design."[24] The emphasis here on Cooper's artistic self-consciousness, and on his sensitivity to contemporary social issues, are valuable supplements to the artist-as-dreamer position. Tompkins is extremely persuasive in developing her view of *The Last of the Mohicans* as "a meditation on *kinds*." It is quite another matter, however, to declare that the novel is the expression of Cooper's conscious "attempt to calculate exactly how much violation or mixing of its fundamental categories a society can bear."[25] To insist on this much intentional precision is to ignore entirely the biographical and textual evidence to which Philbrick and Franklin draw attention. In effect, then, Tompkins properly recuperates the conscious artist and social critic, but at the heavy price of ignoring altogether the Cooper who leads us through what another early observer aptly described as "the visions of a long and feverish dream."[26]

CHAPTER 1

3

We can neither dismiss the arguments at the extremes of this issue nor adopt them in their narrow, unmodified form. The alternative I have proposed acknowledges the weight of the evidence on both sides of the question, and aligns it in the understanding that Cooper and his novel at once know and do not know, clearly perceive and unconsciously dream, what goes on between the covers of *The Last of the Mohicans*. It is a case, as I have suggested, of having things both ways—of looking hard at a wrenching moral dilemma and, at the same time, of turning away.

On one side there can be no doubt that Cooper is at times fully in control of the subversive thrust of his materials. This is quite clearly the case, for example, when Natty Bumppo is first introduced. The scout is discovered midstride in a debate with Chingachgook on the moral issue that most troubled Cooper's contemporaries—the justice of the white dispossession of the Indians. It is noteworthy that both parties to the debate are represented as thoughtful, sober, honest, and entirely worthy men. The discussion is finally rather inconclusive, though it is clear—and remarkable—that Natty loses ground almost from the beginning. To his opening gambit that the Europeans are simply doing what the Indians did before them, Chingachgook replies that the whites have always had an unfair advantage in weaponry. The proud possessor of "kill-deer" can hardly disagree, and in what follows he readily concedes the tragedy of the passing of the proud Mohican tribe. In developing his point of view, Chingachgook is modest and yet properly self-confident, articulate, well balanced, and entirely humane in his perspective on the conflict. Natty, meanwhile, is well meaning in a garrulous sort of way, but so unconsciously condescending in his deference to his friend—"But you are a just man for an Indian!" (33)—that his credibility, and the credibility of his position, are seriously undermined. In all, it seems perfectly clear that the novelist knew what he was up to in this vital opening scene. The issue is too timely, too clearly focussed, and too consistently managed for there to be any doubt on that score.

In bending under the weight of Chingachgook's words, Natty admits that his "people have many ways, of which, as an honest man, [he] can't approve. It is one of their customs," he goes on, "to write in books what they have done and seen, instead of telling them in their villages, where the lie can be given to the face of a cowardly boaster, and the brave soldier can call on his comrades to witness for the truth of his words" (31). This is quite evidently to allow that written history may be biased or downright false, and to acknowledge that such distortion is especially liable to occur in accounts by whites of their military conquests. It is of course sharply ironic that Natty should make this point as the immediate sequel to his opening remarks about the justice of colonial warfare. But his unwitting self-betrayal has a place in Cooper's conscious preoccupation with the strain of prejudice he detects in European historical accounts of conflict in the New World. At the very outset of the narrative, in a footnote to an account of British military failures in the colonies, Cooper notes that the youthful George Washington once "saved the remnants of the British army" from humiliating defeat at the hands of the French and Indians. "It is a circumstance worthy of observation," he goes on, that "while all America rang with his well merited reputation, his name does not occur in any European account of the battle" (31). Later, in condemning the celebrated French commander, the Marquis de Montcalm, for his dishonorable complicity in the massacre at Fort William Henry, he complains that "history, like love, is . . . apt to surround her heroes with an atmosphere of imaginary brightness." Chastising as he does "this weakness on the part of a sister muse," and notwithstanding his withdrawal to what he calls "the proper limits of our own humbler vocation" (180), it is clearly Cooper's objective as a novelist to try to set the historical record straight. It is equally clear, however, that he brought to his task a well-developed suspicion of pretensions to complete historical accuracy, especially in efforts, such as his own, to represent the dispossession of the Indians.

Cooper's attention to verbal nuance is further evidence that he was fully alive to the subtler sources of distortion in the representation of "the Indian problem." David Gamut's surname points with almost comical directness to the narrow singularity of his vocational choice, but it glances even more ironically at the utter lack of scale in his clumsy, ill-sorted outward demeanor. "Gamut" thus announces a contradiction. Upon meeting the angular psalmodist, Natty observes, rather pointedly, that "Christian fashions" in naming "fall far below savage customs in this particular. The biggest coward I ever knew was called Lyon; and his wife, Patience, would scold you out of hearing

CHAPTER 1

in less time than a hunted deer would run a rod. With an Indian 'tis a matter of conscience; what he calls himself, he generally is" (57). Unlike Indian names, which tell the truth about their bearers, English names seem designed to deceive, to conceal moral flaws, and in this they betray a lack of "conscience" in the culture from which they arise. Magua makes a similar point in complaining that "the pale faces are prattling women! They have two words for each thing, while a red skin will make the sound of his voice speak for him" (91). Later Duncan Heyward finds that "the language of the Mohicans was accompanied by gestures so direct and natural" that he has little trouble following it. Natty's English, by contrast, is "obscure; because, from the lingering pride of colour, he rather affected the cold and artificial manner, which characterizes all classes of Anglo-Americans, when unexcited" (198–99). The cultural contrast, and what it suggests about the contemporary crisis in Indian affairs, could not be clearer: Indians are honest, direct, natural; English speakers are sophisticated, corrupt, not to be trusted.

The message in all this is so consistent and unequivocal that we can hardly doubt the novelist's intentions. This is the same Cooper who, in describing the Indians, draws attention to fine but very significant shades of implication—it is the "seemingly inevitable fate of" the Mohicans, he observes, to "disappear before the advances, or it might be termed the inroads of civilisation" (6–7)—and who catches himself in, and elects to dramatize, his own drift into morally loaded word choices: "But Uncas, denying his habits, we had almost said his nature, flew with instinctive delicacy . . . to the assistance of the females" (115). Indeed, this marked sensitivity to the bias of his own verbal promptings is undoubtedly of a piece with Cooper's inclination to view the English language with suspicion. Injustice for the Indian, he saw, could steal all but imperceptibly into the readiest of verbal reflexes.

It is a tribute to the novelist's acuity that he claims no exemption from the subtle moral liabilities of his artistic medium. He seems to glimpse, at moments, that he is afloat with other Americans in the eddies and crosscurrents of their shared language. But such moments of penetration are rare enough in Cooper, as they are in most of us. To have risen to the kind of sustained penetration achieved by Melville in, say, *Benito Cereno*, would have been to relinquish that immersion in his culture's give and take that was the essential key to his audience appeal. Cooper achieves his greatest popularity in *The Last of the Mohicans* because the novel anticipates in its readers an anguished sensitivity to the Indian's plight, and a countering impulse to diminish, if not to neutralize altogether, the painful sense of responsibility for the terrible injustice of the situation. Thus if Cooper rises at moments to an awareness of his entanglement in specific cultural formations, he is rather more often to be found engaged quite unreflectingly in the reinforcement of those constructions. The novel concludes with remarkable moral equanimity, in Tamenund's uncomplaining resignation to the crushing defeat and displacement of his people. Cooper betrays none of Melville's awareness (in *Pierre*, for example) that the playing out of the sentimental romantic plot works to mitigate, and even, for his early reviewers, to submerge the most profoundly unsettling implications of his narrative. Several of the epigraphs to chapters toward the end of the novel are drawn from Shakespeare's comedies, and speak of the novelist's desire to leaven the gravity of the tale with a measure of humor. But in the midst of so much accelerating violence and bloodshed, the tags (especially those from the rustic scenes in *A Midsummer Night's Dream*) may seem to illustrate not the action itself, which is hardly festive or comical, but an impulse to distract attention from it.

In the aggregate, these examples indicate that Cooper was deeply ambivalent in his address to the issue at the center of his most popular novel. His impulse to dramatize the destruction of the Indians was in tension with a countering impulse to turn away from that painful reality. He was acutely aware of the lure of comforting rationalizations, but capable nonetheless of surrender to them. The author of *The Last of the Mohicans*, as I find him, is thus neither a mathematically precise social allegorist nor a dreamer. Rather, he is divided against himself, compelled to look at what he cannot bear fully to see, inclined therefore to repress, to distract, to turn away. My Cooper is quite evidently akin to Leslie Fiedler's "half-conscious framer of legends,"[27] as he is to the novelist portrayed by George Dekker, who operates at levels "presumably unknown to . . . himself," whose "submerged but hardly 'inert'" meanings "get across to most readers, although in a vague and half-conscious fashion."[28] He is related as well to Donald Davie's rather twisted Cooper, who draws Uncas toward Cora for no

CHAPTER 1

evident thematic reasons, but merely that he may consummate the attraction in death. "In fact," Davie elaborates,

> since Cora has to be given a touch of the tar-brush before she can be permitted even a symbolic consummation with her Redskin lover, this thread in the plot leads at once into the murkiest most unsavoury element in Cooper, his attitude to sexual relations and the colour bar. His other heroine, the swooning imbecilic child-bride Alice, is a more ghastly symptom than the worst child-women of Dickens or Thackeray, of a pathologically perverted attitude to sex. If the case were simply that Cooper cannot conceive of sexual relations athwart the colour-bar, there would be no point in making a fuss about it. But the truth is that here, as in *The Prairie* and even in *The Pathfinder,* Cooper's imagination continually plays with the possibility, and invites it in order to repress it hysterically.[29]

Davie's characterization of Cooper's habit of simultaneous advance and retreat is clearly cognate with my own. Nor would I quarrel with his sense that the relationship between Cora and Uncas is at the center of what we may think of as the "problem" of the novel. In framing the issue in terms of the putative eccentricities of Cooper's imagination, however, Davie is much too narrow. The dynamics of repression, as they bear on the erotic and the racial in *The Last of the Mohicans,* are the symptoms of a broadly cultural, not an individual and narrowly sexual, pathology.

4

The competing impulses to see and not to see, I have observed, are doubly manifest in Cooper's accommodation to the literary convention requiring that his romantic plot conclude with the restoration of peace and order symbolized in marriage. The relationship between Duncan Heyward and Alice Munro, with its promise of matrimony and domestic fruition in the clearings, is certainly in compliance with reader expectations on this score. The failure of the romantic involvement between Cora Munro and Uncas is just as clearly a deviation, and draws attention to the enduring fear and hatred that separates white "civilization" from Indian "nature." These romantic pairs may be said to compete for center stage, and for the reader's attention and approval, as the novel closes. We cannot doubt that most of Cooper's contemporaries would have regarded the marriage of Alice and Duncan as a union of racially pure Anglo-Saxons, and therefore as a triumph for civilization. They also may have glimpsed, however fleetingly, that this victory is in some respects a mingled one. Duncan is handsome, courageous, and perfectly earnest in his aspirations to heroism; but his judgment is very erratic, and he is a bumbler, forever tripping up in the contests where real heroes are made. For all of her conspicuous purity, Alice is equally incomplete—not quite "imbecilic," as Davie would have her, but twice described as "infantile" in her "dependency" on Duncan (80, 108). Cooper is usually taken to approve of such invertebrate femininity—Duncan's eyes "fell wistfully on the beautiful form of Alice, who was clinging to his arm with the dependency of an infant"—and yet there can be no denying the suggestion that Alice tends to be a little "thin," just as Duncan is a little "thick."

On the other side, Cora and Uncas are physically quite as prepossessing as Duncan and Alice. He is handsome, vigorous, and notably statuesque in his muscularity; she is much more fully developed than her sister, with "a countenance that was exquisitely regular and dignified, and surpassingly beautiful" (19). They are more poised than their pale counterparts, much clearer in judgment, much more decisive in action. Uncas has little to say, but his silence bespeaks manly stoical reserve and a commendable deference to elders. He is unfailing in his grasp of complex situations and thoroughly heroic in his response to all challenges. Cora is equally resourceful. She sees clearly, speaks with authority, and moves forward boldly when circumstances require it. This darker pair are superior to Alice and Duncan, somehow "meant for each other," and yet doomed, by the terms of the culture's taboo on miscegenation, to fail.

Cooper and his early readers, we are told, were firm believers in the superiority of the Anglo-Saxon "race." Apparently, *The Last of the Mohicans* did not stir any conscious doubts on this score. Yet it is no great strain on the text to read it as an argument *for* racial mixing. This is not to suggest that Cooper intended to write a subversive novel, or that the members of his large and enduring audience imagined they were reading one; yet he did, and thousands read it. The problem, of course, is to reconcile the novel's decidedly subversive dimension with its great popularity. The beginning of a solution, as I have suggested, is to recognize that Cooper and his readers were moved by an unconscious need to have it both ways in the matter. In allowing that Uncas's love for Cora "elevated him far above the intelligence, and advanced him probably centuries before the practices of his nation" (115), the Indian is simultaneously held in and released from his inferior "place." Likewise, in the concluding lamentations of the Delaware maidens, the reader is invited, in clear and very positive terms, to think of Uncas and Cora as a couple united by the will of the Great Spirit in the hereafter. To be sure, the bold thrust of the eulogy is promptly qualified. When he hears the romantic description of "the future prospects of Cora and Uncas," Natty "shook his head, like one who knew the error of their simple creed." And it is happy "for the self-command of both Heyward and Munro," we are assured, that "they knew not the meaning of the wild sounds they heard" (343–44). But while such brief disclaimers render the eulogy "safe," they hardly diminish our sense of the imaginative energy, and the weight of approval, that are everywhere evident in Cooper's stunning vision of unity and peace.

This is emphatically to concur in Davie's view that Cooper's "imagination continually plays with the possibility" of "relations athwart the colour-bar," but to insist at the same time that this recurrent gesture arises out of a prior and very marked cultural ambivalence, not from a perverse corner of the novelist's psyche. Guilt is manifestly at large in this complex reflex, but so is high regard for so-called savage virtues and a concomitant wavering of confidence in the strength and durability—and above all, in the morality—of "civilization." Had he left the romance of Cora and Uncas out of his novel, Cooper could have avoided these seemingly awkward complications. Instead, he thrust the star-crossed pair into the very center of the action, and thereby heightened rather than diminished the tension between guilt and denial at the heart of his material. Cooper thus responded to the impulse, at large in the culture and at work in his own creativity, to express this uncertainty, to play out in fictional terms the need to have it both ways with the Indian problem. The experience of this push-pull, patched over but hardly resolved in the novel's conclusion,[30] is not merely an ingredient in the popularity of *The Last of the Mohicans*, but, I want to argue, integral to it. It is the tense play between admiration and horrified rejection of the Indians, approval for and disappointment with the leading white characters, and, especially, between the impulses to see and not to see, to acknowledge guilt and to deny it, that has given the novel its special hold on generations of American readers.

It is entirely compatible with this view of the novel's dynamics that Cooper's first critics were quick to seize upon the novel's very striking departures, but quite uncertain—in telling sorts of ways—what finally to make of them. The anonymous reviewer for the *New-York Review and Atheneum* goes on at length about Cora's "Creole blood," which "sufficiently accounts," in his view, "for her differing in complexion and character from her fair-haired and bright-eyed sister":

> But what capital points the author meant to make out of this distinction, we confess ourselves obtuse enough not to have discovered. Cora, the eldest sister, is sometimes made to assume all her dignity, when a casual observation suggested the recollection of her descent; but the effect is unpleasant, and in no wise poetical. Munro, the father, when he learns from Duncan Heyward . . . that he is a suitor for Alice, the younger sister, gives vent to a transient paroxysm of indignation, as if he suspected that the young soldier, born in southern latitudes, slighted his elder daughter on account of the sable tinge in her escutcheon. . . . But we cannot discern how the purposes of the fiction can be helped, by the supposition that his preference of her younger sister was in anywise to be ascribed to his prejudice of education against the descendants of negroes. It was natural, too, for Uncas to be more attracted by the fuller proportions and brilliant colour of the noble girl, who was ready, at any moment, to sacrifice herself for the more fragile Alice; but this does not render a frequent, inartificial, and painful allusion to an hereditary taint, at all necessary.[31]

This reviewer is at once fixed by and profoundly resistant to Cooper's tangled treatment of race. His response is perfectly representative of the ambivalence I have described, for he cannot approve of what he finds in *The Last of the Mohicans,* but neither can he leave it alone. He is acutely sensitive to the novel's indictment of American racial prejudice. He even denies what the narrative clearly confirms, that Cora's "sable tinge" influences Duncan's romantic preferences. Not at all surprisingly, his guilty defensiveness renders him incapable of reflection on the broader cultural dynamics that his own response serves so graphically to illustrate. For while the entire passage gives tacit tribute to the galvanizing authority of the novel's racial thematics, it insists in the same breath that such painful preoccupations are offensive to good taste and contribute nothing to the meaning of the story.

CHAPTER 1

W. H. Gardiner, writing in the *North American Review,* displays an identical inability to turn away from what he cannot bring himself fully to confront. "Cora," we read, "is quite a bold young woman, and makes rather free, we think, with the savages. This, probably, she felt the better title to do, in respect of the dark blood which flowed in her own veins." Gardiner faults Cooper for this defect in his heroine, but goes on "to confess, that so far as Cora is concerned, our judgments, like Major Heyward's, may be somewhat biassed. We mean no offence whatever to the colored population of the United States; on the contrary, we have a great esteem for them in certain situations; and we acknowledge it to be a vile and abominable prejudice; but still we have (and cannot help it) a particular dislike to the richness of the negro blood in a heroine." Again we have the fascination with the implication of racial injustice, here rooted in the guilt that issues from surrender to "a vile and abominable prejudice." Conscience, Gardiner acknowledges, is powerless to influence the moral error of his ways. But then, in probing once again his dissatisfaction with "the proud bearing of the ardent and noble minded Cora," he concludes that the defect is not his at all, but hers, and resides in her lack of "grace and ease, gentility of deportment, true delicacy, and unaffected refinement, which properly belong to the sphere of life in which [she is] designed to move." Thus we have Cora's character and the critic's guilt both ways in the space of a few sentences, the contradictions coming to rest, if not to any resolution, in the reiteration of the heroine's failure to exhibit "the true notion of a well bred lady."[32]

I am arguing, then, that Cooper's contemporaries betray in their responses to *The Last of the Mohicans* the same complex dynamics that we have witnessed in the novelist and his novel. To this point the discussion has been focused specifically on patterns of contradiction in the representation of and response to Anglo-Americans and Indians. In effect, I have been trying to answer the questions, why did Cooper raise the specter of miscegenation at the very center of his narrative? and how do we reconcile this subversive element with the novel's great popularity? In response I have argued that the relationship between Cora and Uncas is integral to the success of *The Last of the Mohicans* because it speaks to the profound ambivalence, abroad in the culture during the Age of Jackson, on the Indian question. The deep tension accompanying this issue takes expression in patterns of virtually simultaneous address and denial, seeing and not seeing, with the clear implication that Cooper and his audience could neither confront directly nor fully repress their painful sense of moral responsibility for the destruction of the Native Americans. In drawing Cora and Uncas together, then sacrificing them to Indian violence in a melodramatic finale, with concluding overtones of romantic reunion in some vague hereafter, the novelist conceived an ideal vehicle for the controlled release of urgent but very volatile moral sentiments.

But how, then, does the fact that Cora is a mulatto fit into this analysis? What are we to make of this entirely unforeseen, seemingly arbitrary intrusion into an already complicated racial picture? We may, with Donald Davie, regard it as an errant wrinkle in the novelist's sexual imagination. As we have seen, Cooper's first critics take virtually the same view, condemning Cora's "taint" as a meaningless distraction and a gross lapse in taste. But in dismissing Cora's mixed blood, those same critics actually feature it; they cannot accept what they glimpse in her, and yet neither can they let it go. Their attention is galvanized in this way, I have suggested, because Cora and Uncas are the ideal occasion for the release of the impulse to have things both ways. The critics approach and retreat, admire and condemn, without any apparent uneasiness about their contradictory behavior. But they would not be able to ruminate in this manifestly ambivalent way if Cora were Alice's *full* sister. For it is the fraction of black blood in Cora's veins, as W. H. Gardiner observes, that "explains" her freedom "with the savages." Another of the reviewers makes the same point, allowing that "Uncas would have made a good match for Cora, particularly as she had a little of the blood of a darker race in her veins."[33] We entertain no serious doubt that this writer's apparent liberality turns entirely on the fact that Cora is fractionally, but therefore—by what Mark Twain called a "fiction of [American] law and custom"—entirely black. Cora's black blood "explains" her sexuality; for Cooper and his audience, it makes her sexual, and it makes her sexually attractive to Indians. This "flaw" in Cora enables the novel and its readers to speculate in a positive way, because in a "safe" way, on the racial issue in its more delicate and volatile dimension. Her black blood may be said to liberate the lover in Uncas; it frees Cooper to step outside his comforting assumption that "the native warrior of North America" is "commonly chaste" (5) in his address to white women, just as it frees his audience to admire the handsome young Mohican in his capacity as exotic sexual "other." Take away that trace of Negro blood, and all this would have been inconceivable for a large American audience. Take it away, in other words, and *The Last of the Mohicans* loses its "safe" access to otherwise perilous perspectives on the Indian question.

It is essential to add that the significance of Cora's mixed blood does not neatly terminate in the tacit permission to imagine her in a romantic relationship with Uncas. Having it both ways purchases a temporary imaginative release from strict racial fears, but at the same time it gives rise to behavior that confirms those apprehensions. Thus Cora's mixed blood also enflames Magua's revengeful passion, thereby raising the specter of miscegenation that calls out and "justifies" white fear and violence, and that leads ineluctably to her death, and to the death of Uncas, the last hope of the Mohicans.

Cora has other notable qualities, and they are equally contradictory in their bearing on her fate, precisely because they have their source in what is notable about her "blood." In addition to being "ardent," as W. H. Gardiner puts it, she is "bold" and "proud" and "noble minded"; and she is all of this, Gardiner leaves no doubt, because she is black. Thus the polarizing logic of the pure-white-Alice/ardent-dark-Cora contrast enforces a profoundly subversive enrichment of the latter's character. Because she is white, Alice is sexless and submissive and defenseless—she is infantile. Because she is "black," Cora is sexual *and* independent in her judgment, forthright, fully self-possessed. She is courageously outspoken in persuading Natty to leave her and Alice to the mercy of the Hurons. "Why linger," she questions, with extraordinary sangfroid, "to add to the number of the victims of our merciless enemies?" Natty is at first incredulous: "What answer could we give to Munro, when he asked us, where and how we left his children?" But Cora, perhaps glimpsing the vanity and pointlessness in the scout's "noble" self-sacrifice, suggests quite sensibly that he should tell her father to come promptly to his children's rescue. "There is reason in her words!" Natty concedes, evidently quite taken by surprise. "Chingachgook! Uncas! hear you the talk of the dark-eyed woman!" (78) This is the Cora who recognizes the humanity in Magua, and who admits to herself that her father's "imprudent severity" (103) with the Indian has played a major role in provoking conflict and bloodshed. In this unblinking approach to the truth, Cora displays admirable independence and penetration and moral courage. But her insight cannot have been an entirely comfortable one for her audience, especially as it flies directly in the face of patriarchal power and authority as they are embodied in her father, Duncan, Natty, and other white males in the novel, and as they dominated the tone and content of policy and leadership in the Age of Jackson. It is at this juncture that we witness most directly Cooper's brilliance as a spokesman for the members of his morally troubled American audience. For the black blood in Cora's veins serves the culture that would have it both ways by seeming to "explain" her independent access to unsettling, even subversive points of view, and at the same time by seeming to "justify" the countering impulse to ignore or deny the painful truths that she draws into view. The identical dynamic governs the response to her relationship with Uncas, where we see and un-see, draw out and repress, a similarly galvanizing but deeply troublesome perspective. It is as though the half-conscious uncertainty and moral uneasiness of Cooper's time, having centrally to do with Indians, but bearing as well on race-slavery and gender, is gathered up in the portrait of Cora. Little wonder that the critics were at once attracted and confused and put off by her; little wonder that she had to die.

5

The having it both ways in the response to Cora Munro is closely related to the larger pattern of contradiction in the novel as a whole. At times Cooper seems to control these contradictions and the ironies they give rise to; at other times he is apparently unaware of the contrary implications of his work. One wonders, for example, what Cooper intended in the lines from *The Merchant of Venice* that serve as the epigraph to his novel: "Mislike me not, for my complexion,/The shadowed livery of the burnished sun." In what appears to be its primary reference, to Chingachgook and Uncas, who are referred to directly in the book's title, the tag makes a claim, which the narrative quite evidently supports, for the worth and human dignity of "good" Indians. The link with Uncas is further reinforced by the fact that in Shakespeare's play the lines are spoken by a Moroccan prince who makes suit for Portia's hand. The epigraph thus anticipates the futility of the Mohican's romantic aspiration. But did Cooper reflect on the implications of the lines when they are given to Cora? They may be applied to her frustrated attraction to Heyward, and to the racial considerations that figure in his rejection of her. These words in Cora's mouth may also be construed as an appeal for the reader's attention and fair-mindedness in the face of her painful insights and revelations. The irony that attaches to the assignment of the lines to Cora, thus linking her troubles with those that confront the Mohicans, was not, I think, available to Cooper when he gave them their prominent place in his novel.

The Last of the Mohicans amply confirms James Franklin Beard's astute generalization about Cooper's later novels of social analysis. "For all its wealth of conscious insight," Beard observes, "this fiction is so rich in unintended ambiguities that it persuades the modern reader chiefly of the existence of deep cultural dilemmas whose resolution was coming to seem, even to Cooper, beyond any power of human reason."[34] Beard's critical shrewdness culminates in his suggestion that Cooper was profoundly insightful and yet inclined, perhaps because of the world's perverse intractability, not to see. It was the novelist's penchant for "unintended ambiguities," even as he penetrated to the truth of "deep cultural dilemmas," that equipped him to speak for the thousands of Americans who read and approved of *The Last of the Mohicans*. Something of this tendency to have it both ways may surface in his epigraph. It is at work again in Magua's bitter complaint against the unnatural voracity of his white enemies: "His gluttony makes him sick. God gave him enough, and yet he wants all" (301). There is a large measure of truth in what he says, both as it applies to the narrative itself, and even more emphatically in its address to the moral unrest experienced by Cooper's contemporaries as their leaders set the stage for the brutal removal of the Indians. But, of course, the voice of protest is the voice of the novel's arch villain. The painful truth is here articulated by Magua, the cynical politico, whose devious oratorical strategies are identical to those of the utterly unprincipled demogogues who were, Cooper was convinced, the special plague of popular American democracy.[35] It is hardly surprising that the justice of Magua's protest has been rather slenderly observed.

There is a similar muffling of the potentially subversive in Natty's attempt to reassure Duncan that the Hurons have not raped the Munro sisters. "I know your thoughts," the scout insists, "and shame be it to our colour, that you have reason for them; but he who thinks that even a Mingo would ill treat a woman, unless it be to tomahawk her, knows nothing of Indian nature" (215). The fear that Indians lust after white women is groundless, Natty seems to suggest, save as the reaction of white men to projections of their own violent sexual predilections. This point is confirmed on one side by the simple fact that the girls are not raped, and by the impeccable deportment of Uncas; it is confirmed on the other by the example of Munro, whose older daughter is living testimony to the weakness of white men for women of other, darker complexions. Yet Natty's very pointed suggestion gets no response from his immediate auditors, and none that I know of in the critical response to the novel. This is no doubt in part because of the absurdity of his contention that Indians don't abuse white women *except* with tomahawks. But Natty's obtuseness merely reinforces the resistance to what is so obviously mortifying in his perfectly plausible surmise. It is a case once again of subversive gestures caught in tension with a pull toward the comforting illusions of the status quo.

The ironic contradictions so characteristic of *The Last of the Mohicans*, and so integral to the novel's popularity, find a point of intersection in Cora. She is white yet black, virginal yet fully sexual, attracted and attractive to white and red men alike, a loving, dutiful daughter, and her father's severest critic; she is emphatically a woman, yet in context she is manlike in her independence of judgment and assertiveness; the embodiment and advocate of civilization, she is also the witness to and bearer of its shame. For all of this, Cora is the source of marked uncertainty and discomfort in others. When she first beholds the handsome Uncas, for example, she exclaims: "Who, that looks at this creature of nature, remembers the shade of his skin!" Cora merely expresses what the others must (in some degree) feel, and yet the response of her white companions—"a short, and apparently an embarrassed, silence" (53)—strongly suggests that they are not prepared to acknowledge the bold, for them evidently untoward, implications of her admiring observation. A similar blending of acknowledgment and denial runs through Munro's account of Cora's background. Having prefaced his remarks with copious allusions to his "ancient and honorable family," and to his honor in affairs of the heart, the old soldier describes his duty in the colonial West Indies, where it was his "lot to form a connexion with one who in time became my wife, and the mother of Cora." The word "lot" ascribes to chance what we feel must have been a matter of conscious design in the service of desire. Whether or not Munro knew in advance that Cora's mother was a mulatto is not entirely clear, though his hedging in the matter strongly suggests that he did. But it is unequivocally the case that Munro regards as inherently inferior the mixed blood of the woman he so freely embraced. Miscegenation, he says, "is a curse entailed on Scotland, by her unnatural union with a foreign and trading people." Thus he sidesteps entirely his initiative in the creation of his mulatto daughter, adopting instead the ludicrous position that he is the primary victim of the "curse." Munro may deceive himself here, but his submerged feelings of shame and moral compromise are of course perfectly manifest in his painful straining to conceal them. The absurdity of his position is compounded by his insistence that the younger man should be impartial in the matter of Cora's "race," while he, her father, is so obviously at pains to conceal his own prejudice. Noting that Duncan is from "the south, where these unfortunate beings are considered of a race inferior to your own," he accuses the embarrassed suitor of scorning "to mingle the blood of the Heywards, with one so degraded." Heyward does not protest the hypocrisy of Munro's position, though he is hardly taken in. But in responding to the older man's charge, he retreats to an equally conspicuous evasion of his own: "'Heaven protect me from a prejudice so unworthy of my reason!' returned Duncan, at the same time conscious of such a feeling, and that as deeply rooted as if it had been engrafted in his nature" (159). Munro promptly acquiesces in this falsehood, but only, we can be sure, because his prospective son-in-law has already responded in kind. One good turn deserves another.

Such painful straining to deny the truth about Cora perfectly illustrates the tendency to have things both ways witnessed more generally in *The Last of the Mohicans*. Characteristically, the source of the doubleness is moral equivocation on the score of race; and typically enough, Cora provides the occasion for the uneasy maneuvering. Such numerous intervals in the novel oblige us to reassess the view—widely held among Coopers readers, but here quite memorably expressed by Jane Tompkins—that *The Last of the Mohicans* has "no ambiguities worth shaking a stick at."[36] This generalization hardly squares with the critical evidence assembled here; yet few would deny, I think, that Tompkins speaks for most readers, including scholarly readers, of the novel. My point here should be obvious enough. Reader response to *The Last of the Mohicans* characteristically recapitulates the novel's tendency, and the tendency of its characters, to have things both ways. This is to reiterate that the novel was a great popular success because in it Cooper addressed himself to the issues that most troubled his era, and that his fictional management of those moral dilemmas anticipated rather precisely the habits of simultaneous acknowledgement and denial, seeing and not seeing, of his audience. It is also to suggest that the issues, and the patterns of response to them, have not changed that much over the years.

2

THE VIRGINIAN

1

One of the least plausible developments in *The Virginian* occurs at the very end, when the cowboy hero gets married. Indeed, it is not too much to say that the Virginian actually betrays the myth that he otherwise definitively embodies when he joins Molly Stark Wood in matrimony. In part at least, our response arises out of knowledge, derived from cowboy books and movies, that American heroes of the virile, Western stripe don't get married—they didn't in the tradition that Owen Wister fell heir to, and they haven't in the tradition that he has fostered. But our dismay and incredulity are also reinforced by the text of the novel itself, which seems everywhere compatible with the myth of the bachelor hero except in its untoward conclusion. The narrator never condescends to mention the wedding ceremony, let alone describe it, and his attitude toward the hero as patriarch—"he was an important man, with a strong grip on many various enterprises, and able to give his wife all and more than she asked or desired"[1]—mingles mild irony with a rather stronger brand of indifference. And there is the hero's attitude to consider. He is openly contemptuous of marriage whenever it comes up for comment; and while he claims in one mood that his union with Molly is a dream come true, in another he inadvertently suggests that matrimony may run counter to a deeply regressive strain in his nature. Specifically, as the Virginian and his new wife settle into their perfectly paradisical honeymoon retreat, the groom compares himself to "a little wild animal" that he and Molly observe "out on a small stretch of sand." The

CHAPTER 2

creature "turned its gray head and its pointed black nose this way and that, never seeing them, and then rolled upon its back in the warm dry sand." Finally, it scurries out of sight. "I am like that fellow," ventures the Virginian.

> "I have often done the same." And stretching slowly his arms and legs, he lay full length upon his back, letting his head rest upon her. "If I could talk his animal language I could talk to him," he pursued. "And he would say to me: 'Come and roll on the sands. Where's the use of fretting? What's the gain in being a man? Come roll on the sands with me.' That's what he would say." The Virginian paused. "But," he continued, "the trouble is, I am responsible. If that could only be forgot forever by you and me!" Again he paused and went on, always dreamily. "Often when I have camped here, it has made me want to become the ground, become the water, become the trees, mix with the whole thing. Not know myself from it. Never unmix again. Why is that?" he demanded, looking at her. "What is it? You don't know, nor I don't. I wonder would everybody feel that way here?" (356)

The Virginian never gets answers to his questions; he doesn't even pursue them for long. But it is clear, at least, that the longing he gives voice to has its focus in a desire to withdraw from the responsibilities that fall to him as an adult. In acknowledging this urge to retreat from "experience," he does not raise the prospect of irresponsibility as an alternative. Instead, his implicit wish is to return to innocence, but to a variety of innocence that verges sharply toward oblivion. It is not from knowledge that the hero shrinks, but from consciousness itself; and the implicit trajectory of this impulse bears him toward death, the final respite from the toils of thought. In what follows I want to reflect on a number of questions that arise naturally from this passage. To what extent does the novel afford us an understanding of "the trouble" that the Virginian refers to when he says, "I am responsible"? What is it in his past as the text records it that has so wearied him? And why does this lassitude, this drift toward the imagined comforts of oblivion, overtake him at this particular, very special interval? What is it about a honeymoon, in short, that makes death so appealing to the cowboy?

2

It is part and parcel of the cowboy's culture to be suspicious of marriage. He regards matrimony as all that is artificial, constraining, corrupting and hypocritical in civilization. And being a man who believes in playing by the rules, the Virginian seems to know what the text clearly illustrates—that once he has entered the civilized game, he will pursue it with characteristic energy in its prescribed terms. Thus he holds back. When we first catch sight of him, he is making broad fun of Uncle Hughey's intention to marry. Family life, he suggests, is for the old and impotent. "What with women and children and wire fences," he complains, with others of his kind, the cattle frontier will "not long be a country for men" (69). This aversion to the domestic prompts him to conceive an elaborate baby-switching prank at the Swinton barbecue, and it finds inadvertent expression when his contempt for poor Em'ly gives rise to the practical joke that spells her ultimate undoing. But he is himself the best spokesman for his perspective on this score. "Nothing's queer," he observes, "except marriage and lightning. Them two occurrences can still give me a sensation of surprise" (191).

The cowboy's strong inclination to regard matrimony as a threshold on civilization has an obvious corollary in the deep suspicion and fear of women. As the bearers and enforcers of civilized ways, women are viewed as humorless, grasping, intolerant, and repressed. Most of the Vermont females fulfill this stereotype. Motherhood is equated with sentiment, teething, and the officious domesticity that is ridiculed in the egregious Em'ly. And while the Virginian's evidently wide sexual experience is regarded as the healthy overflow of youthful high spirits, a similar sexual readiness in women is viewed as unnatural, unclean, corrupting. Thus when it becomes apparent that the cowboy hero has had his way with the landlady in Medicine Bow, the narrator crows that "this silent free lance had been easily victorious" (36). The landlady, meanwhile, is held up as an example of devious sexual subtlety: "Impropriety lurked noiselessly all over her. You could not have specified how; it was interblended with her sum total" (33).

Molly is none of these terrible things, of course; but as an attractive, eligible female who has engaged the attention of the Virginian, she is potentially all of them. Little wonder, then, given her manifest potential and his prepossessions, that the description of their courtship is dominated by the language of warfare. Love, especially as Molly experiences it, amounts to a military campaign, complete with tactics and maneuvering, and, of course, an enemy. "It may be said," ventures the narrator, that Molly "was fighting a battle—nay, a campaign. And perhaps this was a hopeful sign for the Virginian (had he but known it), that the girl resorted to allies. She surrounded herself, she steeped herself, with the East, to have, as it were, a sort of counteractant against the spell of the black-haired horseman" (182). Her wiles and his artlessness notwithstanding, it is the cowboy who wins the war. "At the last white-hot edge of ordeal, it was she who renounced, and he who had his way" (359). Or does he? After all, "his way" is here equated with marriage, and that, by code and instinct, the Virginian distrusts.

The vocabulary of warfare, and the tendency to characterize Molly as a shrewd, ruthless warrior in unequal combat with an earnest, unknowing victim, lends very substantial confirmation to the suspicion and fear lodged in the various stereotypes of women in *The Virginian*. Molly's behavior in the courtship has the same effect. Above all else, she is cast as a scheming deceiver. For example, she pretends to be ignorant of the fact that the Virginian is the anonymous horseman who once came to her rescue. She waits for him to open the subject, planning then "to be surprised, and gradually to remember, and finally to be very nice to him" (83–84). The maneuver backfires when the cowboy penetrates her dissimulation and draws it into the open: "Don't you think predentin' yu' don't know a man,—his name's nothin', but *him*,—a man whom you were glad enough to let assist yu' when somebody was needed,—don't you think that's mighty close to hide-and-seek them children plays?" (95). Molly is also a social and cultural snob, unwilling or unable to credit her suitor with the intelligence and judgment and taste that the text ascribes to him. And she is cruel. Arising directly out of the frustration of her schemes and the collapse of virtually all defenses, her cruelty is the reflex of diminishing confidence and power. "She could wound him, and she knew it. Nobody else could. That is why she did it" (183).

Molly Stark Wood is no more or less, of course, than the novel and its audience make her. She is as profoundly a cultural product as her male counterpart; hence, it falls to her to serve as a foil to his estimable qualities as Nature's Nobleman. For his part, he craves space and solitude; for company, when he needs it, he prefers men. He left Virginia as a youngster, and he has no inclination to return: "'This has got into my system.' He swept his hand out at the vast space of the world. 'I went back home to see my folks once. Mother was dyin' slow, and she wanted me. I stayed a year. But the Virginia mountains could please me no more. After she was gone, I told my brothers and sisters good-bye. We like each other well enough, but I reckon I'll not go back.'" (54). It is in the very nature of the cultural fabric from which she is constructed that Molly must manipulate and seduce in order to win this independent, restless, solitary man-child to the side of permanence, family, community—to civilization. It is not in the cards that she should manage to domesticate American Adam without seeming to deceive and corrupt him in the process. The cultural scenario, which evidently informs both the book and the prepossessions we bring to our reading, makes this virtually inevitable.

There is a final element in this survey of the pronounced anticonjugal dimension in the hero and his book. I refer to the narrator. It is no strain on the evidence to advance the notion that the culturally encoded resistance to the union between the handsome hero and the Vermont maiden finds reinforcement in the attitude of the narrator, who emerges as Molly's leading, if unannounced, competitor in love. From the outset he is taken with the Virginian's physical presence. He compares the cowboy's movements to "the undulations of a tiger, smooth and easy, as if his muscles flowed beneath the skin" (2); he observes that his friend's "tiger limberness and his beauty were rich with unabated youth" (49); and he allows that when the Virginian is "clean and dressed and decent," he has "never seen a creature more irresistibly handsome" (177). In fact, there is nothing guarded or demure in the remarkable intensity and specificity of the narrator's expression of romantic ardor. "Had I been a woman," he admits, in admiration of the cowboy's smile, "it would have made me his to do what he pleased with on the spot" (180). Even more to the point: "Had I been the bride, I should have taken the giant [the Virginian], dust and all" (3). Aware as we are of the narrator's inevitable frustration in love, we surmise that he envies Molly her triumph, and that his envy, in turn, flows into and informs the management and tone of his narrative.

3

But if the Virginian has good reasons to second-guess himself on his honeymoon, he has as many good reasons to be pleased with his new estate. For the novel provides him with a copious array of incentives, direct and indirect, to matrimony. The most obvious and direct of these is his passion for Molly. In spite of the code, the narrator, and all that he witnesses in the fair visitor from Vermont, the Virginian courts his beloved with the energy and persistence and resourcefulness of an Elizabethan sonneteer. He falls in love at first sight. He is wounded by Molly, and he burns for her; he submits to her tutelage; he dresses up for her, and he courts her kin. Before he can triumph in love, however, he must be weak and needful and dependent that Molly may be strong. The Virginian is thus absolute for love, and in winning the schoolmarm's hand, he gets precisely what he wants most.

Clearly enough, Molly's is a profoundly ambiguous role. For if she embodies much that the novel characterizes as wrong in civilization, she is at the same time a powerful representative of its attractions. Nature and the "natural" condition, as Wister portrays them, are similarly ambiguous and have an equally divided relation to the cowboy. The image of the great outdoors and the simple, all-male life of individual freedom and self-sufficiency is undoubtedly a very positive force in *The Virginian*. But the same setting and circumstances sometimes give rise to varieties of disorder and violence that pose a serious challenge to human purposes. It is a major part of the Virginian's charge as the Judge's foreman to keep the men under control. This is exhausting work, a heavy tax on nerves and good humor and a drain on reserves of physical strength. Responsibility of this sort, which he assumes with almost painful pride and dedication, no doubt figures in the fatigue that the Virginian describes to Molly on their honeymoon.

But his weariness, the text strongly suggests, is more spiritual and moral than physical. This skillful leader and fearless gunfighter wins the respect of his peers, and of the narrator, because he is, above all else, a master "at the cool art of self-preservation" (21). Such mastery arises out of a convergence of traditional American values, especially individualism, with an awkwardly contrasting array of "Darwinian" notions bearing on race and survival. The result is a standard of male behavior that equates virtue with the silent control of emotion and the possession of physical power. Life is war; regeneration is frequently to be found in violence. The struggle for survival, or "equality," finds its purest, most dramatic (and exciting) expression in combat to the death between two men—the duel. The code is fundamentally amoral; it honors fair play and its legitimate enforcement, but it bows down to, depends on, and deeply relishes the authority of force.[2]

"A man must take care of himself" is the hard first principle of cowboy heroism. Its observance figures prominently in the Virginian's preeminence, just as it informs his "hands-off" attitude to most of the injustice that he witnesses in the world around him. It is a harsh code, and the romantic individualism that it fosters and celebrates has its price in a spectacle of unredeemed violence and suffering. The romance is conspicuous enough in the cowboy, but so is the cost. When he comes upon the warm corpse of the hapless, just murdered Shorty, for example, he observes: "There was no natural harm in him. . . . But you must do a thing well in this country" (303). Shorty dies not because he is an immoral person, but because he is weak, inadequate, without the requisite resources in the "art of self-preservation." The Virginian recognizes this, and he responds, as the code says he must, by allowing Nature to take her course. This obligation to remain passive in the face of what is regarded as necessary or inevitable is the source of deep melancholy in the Virginian. It is a terrible weight on his human resilience to stand by as the likes of Balaam and Trampas brutalize innocent men and animals. The weight of the burden is increased by the fact that the irresistible forces of Nature strike suddenly and frequently. Thus in looking at poor Shorty, the Virginian seems to behold an endless procession of innocent but doomed weaklings: "There was not a line of badness in the face; yet also there was not a line of strength; no promise in the eye, or nose, or chin; the whole thing melted to a stubby, featureless mediocrity. It was a countenance like thousands; and hopelessness filled the Virginian as he looked at this lost dog, and his dull, wistful eyes" (194).

The cruelty written so boldly through the natural scheme of things is made even more depressing for the Virginian when his sense of professional responsibility is drawn into painful conflict with deep personal attachments. Rustling is on the rise along the cattle frontier, and it falls to the Judge's foreman to combat the problem. In the course of duty, he is obliged to participate in the lynching of two rustlers, one of whom is his old friend, Steve. The narrator, civilized man that he is, shrinks "from any contact with what they were doing," though he assumes that the cowboy's "wholesome frontier nerves knew nothing of such refinement" (275–76). In fact, though the Virginian insists again and again on the justice of the thing, the gravity of his deed is borne home to him by Steve's refusal to speak to him just before the end. On one side, he insists that "a man goes through with his responsibilities" (285); on the other; he is haunted by the image of his friend, "dangling back in the cottonwoods" (286). The narrator reasons, "Did you want endorsement from the man you were hanging? That's asking a little too much" (287). But reasoning has no effect on the crumbling hero, who gives way to tears and later compares himself to "a little boy sleepin' . . . that still keeps his fear of the dark" (300). Stretched to the limit of his tolerance for frontier justice, he feels small and alien:

> "I'll be pretty near glad when we get out of these mountains," said the Virginian. "They're most too big."
> The pines had altogether ceased; but their silence was as tremendous as their roar had been.
> "I don't know, though," he resumed. "There's times when the plains can be awful big, too." (296)

Later, when Steve's message of friendship and reconciliation comes to light, the cowboy is restored to his former self. But this does nothing to obscure the fact that he has bent and even cracked under the harsh code of survival.

It would be misleading to argue that it is the simple cruelty of the West that brings the Virginian to his knees. In fact, he buckles under the pressure of a rather more complicated moral burden. It is symptomatic that he seems unsure whether to regard Steve as a criminal or simply an incompetent, that is, whether his mistake was the moral one of rustling or the merely practical one of getting caught. "Now back East," lectures the narrator, "you can be middling and get along. But if you go to try a thing on in this Western country, you've got to do it *well*. You've got to deal cards *well*; you've got to steal *well*; and if you claim to be quick with your gun, you must be quick, for you're a public temptation, and some man will not resist trying to prove he is the quicker. You must break all the Commandments *well* in this Western country" (288). The little sermon is explicit: if you are going to survive in the West, you must operate efficiently outside of the law. Indeed, there is an ample measure of pride stirred into this heroic, if thoroughly un-Christian, code, for the Virginian is a master gambler and gunman. Stealing is of course the commandment that Steve does not break well enough to survive. Thus it is clearly implied that Steve's rustling is no more a moral issue than his friend's poker and dueling. The Virginian's decision to shoot it out with Trampas derives its legitimacy from a code of survival that is glamourous largely because it is extralegal. As the narrator reassures us, "It is only the great mediocrity that goes to law in these personal matters" (334). The game, whether it involves cards or pistols or somebody else's cattle, is good precisely because it violates civilized laws. Thus conventional morality is at issue only to the extent that it is disregarded. The simple point of the game is success—victory, survival—and where the handsome hero always comes out on top, his friend Steve loses once, and for good.

The problem for the Virginian in the lynching arises out of the fact that his natural code is also preeminently an individual and personal scheme of values. He is happy enough, of course, to take credit for the execution of Trampas, but it is quite another thing to bear personal responsibility for the hanging of a friend who is, in terms of the code, much less villain than amiable fool. When the Virginian again and again protests the justice of the lynching—"I would do it all over again the same this morning. Just the same" (283)—he shows evidence of retreat from the heroic code of individual survival to a civilized rule of law. At one level the cowboy-hangman is anxious to share the responsibility for Steve's death with the community at large. This is the Judge's sense of things as he defends the hero's behavior to Molly. When the arm of the law is as weak as it is on the frontier, he insists, vigilantism is "far from being a *defiance* of the law," rather, "it is an *assertion* of it—the fundamental assertion of self-governing men, upon whom our whole social fabric is based" (314). Thus the "social fabric" serves well enough to carry the weight of personal responsibility for Steve's death that the Virginian labors under. At another level, however, the immunity that civilized justice affords the executioner is incompatible with his need for confirmation of personal friendship within a code of manly struggle that transcends mere laws. As the narrator says, you can't expect your friends to like it when you hang them. To be consistent in the matter, the Virginian must give up the natural code that binds him to Steve, and that accounts for his anguish after the lynching, or he must align himself completely with the civilized rule of law that ameliorates the heavy burden of responsibility but cuts him off from the old friends and old ways. Either course has advantages and flaws, but having it both ways, as the Virginian's moral collapse well illustrates, is unbearable.

4

And yet, in a very real and painful sense, it is precisely his cultural condition to have it both ways. True, the Virginian *finally* decides for civilization. But not before he has made it indelibly clear that he is willing to gamble Molly and all that she represents against his impulse to do what a man's got to do, outside the law, in the duel with Trampas. Only when his reputation as a survivor is secure does he return to the place at Molly's side, as husband, father, Western entrepreneur. There is no reason to suppose that the old ways have lost their deep hold on him, just because he has crossed the line. Nor need we suppose that the cowboy is entirely resigned to matrimony just because he has entered it. To the contrary, we began by observing that marriage and domestic life are as imperfectly adjusted to the Virginian's "identity" as they are to our expectations of him. Yet the harsh code of Nature, which honors individual survivors but not weaklings, and not even friends, doesn't completely suit him or us either. On both sides of the nearly palpable line separating the natural from the civilized, there is a portion of discomfort for the heroic horseman from the plains. He recoils by instinct from what he regards as soft, hypocritical, and corrupting in women and marriage, but he is also fatigued and ultimately repelled by the inhuman terms of the code. In fact, he waffles. Molly and her civilization look good to him after the lynching, but a shoot-out with Trampas seems morally obligatory the day before his wedding.

The Virginian vacillates because he is ambivalent, and the prospect of endless vacillation is the key to the discontent that he gives voice to on his honeymoon. He acknowledges a desire to join company with the "little wild animal" that seems to say, "Where's the use of fretting? What's the gain in being a man?" But although he craves the freedom from care that he attributes to the small creature, he also recognizes that such contentment will always elude him. "The trouble is," he complains, "I am responsible." It is part and parcel of his humanity that he should attempt to locate and abide by a coherent, ultimately constructive scheme of values. But given his demonstrated ambivalence to both world views available to him, it is hardly surprising that the Virginian should equate being "responsible" with "trouble." His longing for the certitude and stability and continuity requisite to "responsible" behavior is utterly frustrated, he senses, by the qualities of mind that he brings to their pursuit. He seems to glimpse that all human circumstances open to him, even honeymoons, are subject to the erosive influence of his ambivalence. Having thus located the source of his disenchantment in his own divided perspective on the world, he turns for relief, naturally enough, to the oblivion that he imagines the "little wild animal" enjoys.

This is, I grant, to make a great deal out of a single paragraph. But if the mood that descends on the cowboy is brief and rather obscure, it is nonetheless potent with implication. In fact, he is overtaken by the lure of death on one other occasion in the novel, when he comes momentarily to consciousness after having been ambushed. For some reason, he feels compelled to tell Molly, who has come to his aid, what has just passed through his literally unconscious mind:

> "I thought they had found me. I expected they were going to kill me." He stopped, and she gave him more of the hot drink, which he took, still lying and looking at her as if the present did not reach his senses. "I knew hands were touching me. I reckon I was not dead. I knew about them soon as they began, only I could not interfere." He waited again. "It is mighty strange where I have been. No. Mighty natural." (236)

The ambivalence here is precisely poised. On one side, the cowboy properly locates his suffering in a context of violence and the code of survival. On the other, he finds himself in the care of the civilized gentlewoman he wants to marry. But neither of the worlds present to his consciousness is equal to the task of drawing his attention away from the margins of oblivion and death that he finds so "natural" and appealing. Like the honeymoon meditation, this passage lends support to the conclusion that there are, after all, not two, but three competing dimensions to the Virginian's interior life. There is a strong pull toward the natural code; there is the promise of civilization; and, emergent from the fatigue and frustration that their incompatibility engenders, there is a tertium quid, a longing for retreat to a condition imagined to antedate tension and discord and ambivalence. This condition is primarily a state of mind, specifically of innocence, but its temporal placement in the past, its spatial location in a pastoral Eden, and the impulse to return to it, place the hero on an imaginative trajectory that points backward through childhood and infancy to all that is implied in his ambition "to become the ground, become the water, become the trees, mix with the whole thing. Not know myself from it. Never unmix again." Though direct and simple in its thrust, this third dimension to the cowboy's consciousness is no doubt very complex in its origins and operations. At the very least, however, we may define it as a longing for simplicity and peace borne out of an identifiably American struggle to come to terms with nature, sex, women, men, marriage, violence, domesticity, the law. In his possession of this familiar cultural reflex, the Virginian takes his place alongside Natty Bumppo, Huckleberry Finn, Isaac McCaslin, and a procession of lesser American heroes who recoil from life as they find it in the new world, and retreat toward something as old and simple and pure as death itself.

5

The enduring popularity of *The Virginian*, and the grand literary progeny that it has fostered, are evidence that the hero's condition speaks emphatically to our own. I would venture that the resonance of this novel derives to a significant extent from its dramatization of key areas of tension in our national culture. More specifically, this manifestly fictional cowboy is real for us because his dual, incomplete, and finally incompatible allegiances to the natural and the civilized mirror our own. Having said this much, however, it is essential to add that *The Virginian* is not generally taken to be a novel in which all paths to resolution are blocked. The notion advanced here, that the cowboy suffers under the strain of unresolved contradictions, runs counter to received critical opinion. Gary Scharnhorst ably summarizes the consensus view—also advanced by David Brion Davis, Neal Lambert, and John G. Cawelti—that Wister's hero is "a figure who transcended various cultural conflicts."[3] There can be little quarrel, I think, with the view that Wister thought of his handsome cowboy as a blend of the best qualities commonly associated with East and West, or with nature and civilization. The evidence on this score is impressive. Still, as I hope I have shown, there is also a strong countering tendency at large in the novel. Wister's plan for the transcendence of conflict competes with a less conscious impulse to undermine the happy union of opposites. It is this latter, emergent Wister who subverts both the heroic and the domestic options available to the Virginian, dramatizes the cowboy's regressive reaction to the impasse, and offers ground for the view that his final acquiescence in marriage is a flabby compromise.

In effect, the novel has it both ways. So, I want to argue, does the reader. Indeed, it is the key to the success of *The Virginian* that it enables the reader to have the Virginian both ways, as the ruggedly individualistic American Adam and as the natural Western gentleman and paterfamilias, even as it insists that the two roles are fundamentally incompatible. The text brings us face to face with a major cultural tension between male and domestic ideals, and then, without resolving that tension, it somehow diminishes it to a point of virtual invisibility. But the conflict is not transcended; it is simply evaded. The novel's subversive drift is not eclipsed or concealed; rather, it is passed over. We are aware, after all, of the hero's discontents; we are witness to the untoward reflections that overtake him on his honeymoon. But readers are strongly inclined, with Wister, to minimize these elements of discord. As the critical consensus clearly suggests, we have been quite successful at eclipsing them from sight and mind.

In my final chapter I will look much more carefully at this matter of having it both ways. For now, let me suggest at least that the false resolution of tension, the tacit refusal to come to terms with the meaning of the cowboy's retreat from his destiny, permits Wister, as it permits us, to endure stubborn contradiction with relative equanimity. Our culture seems to endorse such evasions. Indeed, the popularity of *The Virginian*, and of the formula it embodies, are signal evidence on this score. It is of course possible to read the novel as an endorsement of the happy union between the values of East and West, women and men, civilization and nature. The text clearly supports this interpretation; Wister had something very like this in mind. But it is also necessary to acknowledge that something else, something restlessly contradictory, is going on between the covers of this famous book. Viewed from this less familiar perspective, the novel is not about the success of compromise, but about its failure. Or more accurately perhaps, it is a novel that cultivates an illusion of resolution at the same time that it gives play, less centrally and emphatically, to elements of discord. This is not, it is essential to stress, a case of conspicuous omission. Rather, it is a matter of seeing and not seeing at the same time. The novel thus dramatizes its own evasiveness, just as it provides the reader with evidence of a cognate impulse to have things both ways. This happens, I will argue in more detail later on, because we want it to—or because our culture, which we at once receive and endorse, wants it to. We see and fail to see at the same time, just as Wister did, because it suits our purposes to do so. The alternative, a vigilant readiness to acknowledge all contradiction, would have its price in a painful diminishment of our world. It would also make *The Virginian* a much less popular book.

3
THE SEA-WOLF

1

A recent surge of scholarly interest in Jack London's *The Sea-Wolf* gives evidence of an emergent critical consensus in several major areas of discussion, but of a marked division of opinion in matters of detail. Increased attention to the novel indicates that its high status in the London canon is secure, and that London's standing with the academic establishment—often uncertain in the past—has moved to a broader, firmer footing. Additionally, there is agreement among virtually all recent critics that the novel is significantly autobiographical in nature. Not surprisingly, the lines drawn between the facts of London's life and the details of his fiction vary from one observer to another, but the existence of such lines is never seriously questioned. There is general consent as well to the notion that *The Sea-Wolf* serves as a vehicle for one or more major strands of thought, sometimes referred to as Jack London's "philosophy." Again, there is some disagreement at more specific levels of interpretation. For example, Clarice Stasz argues forcefully that the novel figures prominently in Jack London's progressive critique of turn-of-the-century sex roles. Taking a much different tack, Joan D. Hedrick insists that the novel is a failed analysis of the brutalizing degradation of the masses in capitalist society. Meanwhile, Susan Ward finds that London's narrative successfully merges "serious" materials drawn from Darwin, Spencer, Marx, and Nietzsche with a popular, romantic love story. Such variety in approach and emphasis notwithstanding, these essays and others like them clearly agree that *The Sea-Wolf* is a novel of ideas.[1]

There is equally broad-based assent to the view that London's maritime narrative is richly psychological in design and implication. The author's fascinating, complex sexuality is almost invariably drawn into the critical foreground, though the array and deployment of sexual ingredients observed in the writer and the work vary quite considerably. Robert Forrey strongly emphasizes evidence of repressed homosexuality in both the novelist and the novel, whereas Jon A. Yoder stresses London's frustrated, bibulous male chauvinism.[2] The most broadly conceived, and perhaps the most generally persuasive, of the recent essays in this psychological vein is Charles N. Watson, Jr.'s "Sexual Conflict in *The Sea-Wolf.*" Allowing that the novel's pronounced ambivalences in sexual matters "have their origin in London's own sexual nature," Watson nonetheless moves quickly from biographical speculation to textual issues as they emerge from "the principle triangle of relationships in *The Sea-Wolf.*" Watson approaches the novel as the record of an initiation in which "Humphrey Van Weyden is torn between the 'masculine' Wolf Larsen and the 'feminine' Maud Brewster. In this conflict the 'masculine' implies both homosexuality and nihilism (the creed of brute strength), while the "feminine" implies a combination of heterosexuality and ethical idealism. Thus, the central action of the novel—the midpoint of Humphrey's development—involves a crisis of sexual as well as intellectual orientation. Emerging from an abnormally prolonged stage of mother-dependency, Humphrey must pass through an intermediate stage of masculine exclusivity to a final stage of sexual and philosophical adulthood."[3]

I conclude this summary of recent criticism with a relatively close look at Watson's essay not only because his general line of analysis strikes me as lucid and plausible, but also because it echoes quite faithfully a final area of critical consensus that opens directly on my topic. Specifically, while he argues that Maud Brewster's sudden appearance "in mid-ocean" is "readily justified in the light of her vital role in Humphrey's psychological development," Watson also recognizes the "literal improbability" of her advent and acknowledges "the frequent charge" that the love story that dominates after Maud's arrival may be "sentimental nonsense."[4] In general terms Watson's analysis reflects the view held by most critics, first and most vigorously expressed by Ambrose Bierce in a letter to George Sterling: "The love element, with its absurd suppressions and impossible proprieties, is awful." Many readers may not share the vehemence of Bierce's "overwhelming contempt for the sexless lovers,"[5] but there is virtually unanimous agreement that *The Sea-Wolf* is most engaging in the exclusively male sections before "the twittering Maud Brewster" sets foot on the *Ghost*. The scornful epithet is Franklin Walker's,[6] but the contempt that it expresses has fallen ceaselessly on the head of poor Maud Brewster. With her arrival, argues Watson, the narrative is overtaken by a "saccharine conventionality" that "unquestionably robs the last third of the novel of much of its power." John Perry is of similar mind, but rather blunter: "After Larsen dies . . . the novel degenerates into pure literary bosh." He imagines the Van Weydens living "happily ever after, correcting each other's proofs." Forrey finds Maud "an unbelievable, bloodless character," and Hedrick describes her, with conspicuous impatience, as "elegant and insufferable," "a good little mother" who exchanges with Humphrey, "at greater length than the reader would wish—the banalities of their sentimental love." Stasz and Ward perceive in Maud a somewhat more balanced array of qualities, aligning her with moral principle, spirituality, social idealism, and London's notion of "the mate-woman." As the correlative of her virtue, however, they find her slender ("the most ethereal and idealized of all London's female characters") and, "in keeping with nineteenth-century fictional convention," utterly subordinate to the male protagonists.[7]

Although the sheer weight of consensus on the score of Maud Brewster is certainly clear, and perhaps readily understood, there is some cause, I believe, to review the textual evidence upon which any such judgment must be based. In what follows I will scrutinize the characterization of Maud in order to test the common view that she is a "twittering" female. I take it as my thesis that the heroine of *The Sea-Wolf* is a much more distinctive and sophisticated and forceful character than her fictional companions, and the critics, have recognized. There are ironies that attach to this failure of critical penetration; and the characteristic condescension to Maud can be seen as cognate with larger warps in understanding. I want to suggest, in other words, that a reassessment of Maud Brewster, though in itself a relatively narrow undertaking, may open up fresh perspectives on the novel as a whole, and on the culture in which it has flourished as a perennial popular classic.

CHAPTER 3

2

Joan D. Hedrick speaks for a host of critics and numberless readers in finding that *The Sea-Wolf* enforces "a choice between the man's world of raw power and the woman's world of poetry and 'culture,' a choice between Wolf Larsen and Maud Brewster."[8] The consensus that this assertion articulates is doubly remarkable. In the first place, one cannot fail to be struck by the fact that the contrast between extreme stereotypes of gender should lead irresistibly and directly to the necessity for choice. It appears that this juxtaposition of male and female types is so heavily laden with cultural freight that its witnesses are powerless to reserve judgment or to consider more balanced alternatives, but instead respond reflexively by seizing on one extreme or the other. Second, if we are a little uneasy with the apparent cultural authority of such a radical polarization of male and female images, then we will be even more unsettled when we recognize that the consensus construction of the obligatory "choice" results from a curiously selective treatment of textual evidence. In other words, a cultural habituation to polarized gender stereotypes has informed—or, as I will argue, misinformed—the critical perception of the text. This predisposition to extremes is especially pronounced in the standard critical view of Maud Brewster.

The response to Maud, ranging from faint praise to outright contempt, has its source in the perception that she is a conventional, repressed Victorian prude whose totally sublimated libido renders her frail, dependent, poetic ("twittering"), sexless, and therefore, by some familiar but nonetheless peculiar brand of logic, "cultured." To the extent that its artistic design is compatible with absolute reliability in such matters, the text of *The Sea-Wolf* tells us that Maud is at once none of this and much more than this. The text is perfectly unequivocal in describing Maud's enthusiasm for clubbing seals to death. To be sure, her primitive vigor is mingled with a rough kind of sportsmanship; thus whenever a seal "looked tired and lagged, she let it slip past. But I noticed, also, whenever one, with a show of fight, tried to break past, that her eyes glinted and showed bright, and she rapped it smartly with her club. 'My, it's exciting!' she cried, pausing from sheer weakness."[9] And lest we conclude that this upsurge of predatory gusto is totally without foundation in Maud's experience, the text gives clear evidence that she is a longstanding disciple of David Starr

Jordan and his muscular philosophy of the strenuous life and Anglo-Saxon superiority. Maud's readiness for seal killing derives, she says, from her reading in Jordan; and she assures Humphrey that the dynamic president of Stanford University has been a leading influence on her values and behavior:

> "When I dismantled my old Pantheon and cast out Napoleon and Caesar and their fellows, I straightaway erected a new Pantheon," she answered gravely, "and the first I installed was Dr. Jordan."
> "A modern hero."
> "And a greater because modern," she added. "How can the Old World heroes compare with ours!" (243)[10]

It is hero worship of this animated cast, in combination with her native energy and aggressiveness, that brings Maud so readily into Wolf Larsen's orbit. Something quite the opposite of the conventional is at work in her conscious and unembarrassed attraction to the brutally virile captain of the *Ghost*. It is evident from the moment of her arrival on board the schooner that she is deeply responsive to Wolf Larsen's magnetism. Her sensitivity to his vibrant energy is so acute that she is aware of his proximity to Endeavor Island *before* he has actually arrived. A similar responsiveness informs Maud's verbal exchanges with Larsen. This is especially the case during their climatic debates on the nature of love, in which Maud takes arms against the captain's resolute materialism. Her face, Humphrey observes, was one "that rarely displayed color, but to-night it was flushed and vivacious. Her wit was playing keenly, and she was enjoying the tilt as much as Wolf Larsen, and he was enjoying it hugely" (173). For both parties, it seems evident, the discussion has more to do with the release of convergent passion than with the articulation of philosophical differences. Thus when Maud whispers to Larsen, "You are Lucifer" (175), and then steps out of the cabin, it is clear that she is deeply of the Devil's party, and that she knows it.

It is equally clear that Humphrey does *not* know it. His failure to properly gauge Maud's mood is evident in his declaration that she is overcome by an "unnamable and unmistakable terror" (175) as she utters her parting words to Larsen. If Maud is terrified at all, then we must imagine that her fear is largely directed to the intensity of her own attraction to Larsen. But she is also excited—"flushed and vivacious"—and what Humphrey interprets as fear must have some

CHAPTER 3

foundation in her feeling of exhilaration at the discovery of a human spirit that at once stimulates and answers her own. This is not to romanticize in the slightest the sexual predator in Wolf Larsen. It is merely to point out that Humphrey's inclination to find Maud fearful tells us at least as much about him as it does about her. This is once again the case when, at another point in the story, Humphrey observes that Maud is "greatly perturbed" as she and Larsen approach: "She made some idle remark, looking at me, and laughed lightly enough; but I saw her eyes return to his, involuntarily, as though fascinated; then they fell, but not swiftly enough to veil the rush of terror that filled them" (149). Again, "terror" is much too narrow a word, for it fails to register the fascination and surrender in Maud's response to her companion. Her mood makes fuller sense to us when we go on to read that Larsen's eyes, "ordinarily gray and cold and harsh," were now "golden" and "enticing and masterful, [and] at the same time luring and compelling, and speaking a demand and clamor of the blood which no woman, much less Maud Brewster, could misunderstand" (150). Maud knows, and Humphrey seems to recognize, that the situation is supercharged with sexual energy. To be sure, Maud's evident excitement must have fear as one of its ingredients, but to characterize Maud as merely fearful is to flatten the complex tonality of her emotion.[11]

As I have already suggested, we can begin to account for the reductive inadequacy of the descriptive language by turning from its object, Maud, to its source, Humphrey. As her social and cultural peer, her admirer, protector, and prospective husband, Humphrey Van Weyden may strike us as ideally situated to provide a comprehensive, sympathetic portrait of Maud Brewster. Indeed, the general tendency to fault the characterization of Maud is strong evidence that readers have found Humphrey fair and credible. In fact, however, Humphrey's perspective on his future mate is obstructed and distorted in two closely related ways. Most obviously, perhaps, Humphrey's impressions of Maud are powerfully influenced by his feelings for Wolf Larsen. In the second of the episodes just discussed, for example, Humphrey's attention to Maud's "terror" follows as the direct sequel to a detailed portrait of her companion, Wolf Larsen: "He was splendidly muscled, a heavy man, and though he strode with the certitude and directness of the physical man, there was nothing heavy about his stride. The jungle and the wilderness lurked in the uplift and downput of his feet. He was cat-footed, and lithe, and strong, always strong. I likened him to some great tiger, a beast of prowess and prey. He looked it, and the piercing glitter that arose at times in his eyes was the same piercing glitter I had observed in the eyes of caged leopards and other preying creatures of the wild" (149). The homoeroticism of the passage requires little in the way of comment; the admiring Van Weyden is quite evidently fascinated with and powerfully attracted to the man he describes. He draws his attention away from Larsen long enough to describe Maud's marked perturbation, and then returns, with Maud, to gaze upon the captain's amorous eyes. So alluring is Larsen's glance that it triggers in Humphrey precisely the same response that he has just ascribed to Maud. Her "own terror rushed upon me," he reports, "and in that moment of fear,—the most terrible fear a man can experience,—I knew that in inexpressible ways she was dear to me. The knowledge that I loved her rushed upon me with the terror, and with both emotions gripping at my heart and causing my blood at the same time to chill and to leap riotously, I felt myself drawn by a power without me and beyond me, and found my eyes returning against my will to gaze into the eyes of Wolf Larsen" (150).

A fully satisfactory analysis of Humphrey's sometimes baffling state of mind is not easily achieved. At the least, however, it seems safe to say that his sexual attraction to Larsen is at once powerfully resurgent and utterly unacceptable to consciousness. He eases the tension arising from these contradictory tendencies by retreating to the illusion that Maud is the object of his erotic attention, and by imagining that his own fear of Larsen's sexual authority merely echoes the "terror" that he observes in Maud, and in fact projects upon her. This construction of the situation, though conspicuous in its distortions, is brilliant in its overall psychological economy. Maud is rather tepidly "dear" to Humphrey at this early stage in their acquaintance, but the illusion of an attraction to her functions to draw attention away from his obsession with Larsen, and to suggest that his preoccupation with the captain is the outgrowth of his obligations as Maud's anxious lover. In concert with these notions about his own feelings, Humphrey takes it for granted that Maud is as headlong and undistracted in her esteem for him as he supposes he is for her. This assumption has a dual function in his fabricated scheme of things. It reinforces his sense of himself as a virile and protecting male, thus serving to

CHAPTER 3

ease emergent misgivings about his attraction to Larsen, and it lends plausibility to the view that Maud responds to Larsen with simple "terror," thus serving Humphrey's unconscious ambition to remove her from the field of amorous competition. After all, if Maud is merely afraid of the captain, then she can have no interest in competing for his attention. As it is, of course, she competes quite well. But because Humphrey cannot consciously accept his own attraction to Larsen, he cannot face Maud's either. Instead, he imagines himself thrust together with Maud in a conventional heterosexual dyad, offering terrified but valiant resistance to the intrusions of a predatory brute.

If a barely contained erotic attraction to Wolf Larsen works in the immediate foreground to limit and obstruct Humphrey's perception of Maud Brewster, then his general attitude toward women and femininity forms the background to the same phenomenon. This second obstruction to a clear-eyed perspective on Maud has its foundation in Humphrey's history of dependence on maternal figures for comfort and culture, and in a potently reactive inclination to view women as soft, weak, helpless, and fearful. One pole of this ambivalence disposes Humphrey to stand in fear and contempt of what he perceives to be the hypertrophy of the feminine component in his own makeup. Indeed, the very first episode in *The Sea-Wolf* features Humphrey's extraordinary reaction to his own panic aboard the sinking *Martinez*. It was "the screaming of the women, that most tried my nerves," he recalls: "I realized I was becoming hysterical myself; for these were women of my own kind, like my mother and sisters, with the fear of death upon them and unwilling to die. And I remember that the sounds they made reminded me of the squealing of pigs under the knife of the butcher, and I was struck with horror at the vividness of the analogy."(7). Possessed as he is of such disgust and contempt for what he considers the feminine in himself, it is little wonder that Humphrey reacts as he does to Wolf Larsen, and that he learns to enjoy life in the company of men at sea. It was during the period "between the death of Johansen and the arrival on the sealing grounds," he recalls, "that I passed my pleasantest hours on the *Ghost*. . . . During that brief time I was proud of myself, and I grew to love the heave and roll of the *Ghost* under my feet" (103–4). When this interval of relative happiness and growth is interrupted by Maud Brewster, she appears to Humphrey "a being from another world." She reminds him "what a delicate, fragile creature a woman is," and he marvels at the "smallness and softness" of her arms. This pronounced condescension is the direct reflex of Humphrey's proud masculinity, but as such it is also an oblique manifestation of his deeply ingrained contempt for feminine frailty. When we observe Humphrey "bustl[ing] about in quite housewifely fashion" (126), we may be sure that he has not outgrown those feminine proclivities that he fears and despises in himself, and that Maud's arrival on the *Ghost* has evidently revived. Thus Humphrey's rather baffled admission that he is "strangely afraid of this woman" (125) should come as little surprise. After all, Maud is a direct threat, both as sexual competition and as a reminder of what he has suppressed in himself, to Humphrey's delicate psychological equilibrium. In response he fabricates an image of Maud as so "ethereally slender and delicate" (125) that it serves to reinforce, by contrast, his precarious manhood while lending a veneer of plausibility to his insistence that she responds with simple "terror" to Wolf Larsen.

To argue, as I have, that Humphrey's characterization of Maud Brewster cannot be properly understood in separation from the idiosyncratic imperatives of his interior life is, willy-nilly, to throw open the much larger question of narrative point of view in *The Sea-Wolf*. It is not my intention to continue to pursue this important question here, though it may be just as well to underscore my sense that the tone and structure of this narrative are directly and everywhere the mirror of Humphrey's complex, often baffling, construction of reality. Nor is this to deny that many interpretations of the novel involve an awareness of Humphrey's suppressions and exaggerations. For example, when Robert Forrey argues that "the only true passion in the novel is Van Weyden's feelings for Larsen,"[12] he has quite obviously taken the measure of the narrator's repeated assertions of love for Maud. But Forrey's failure to notice that Maud Brewster's feelings for Larsen are, in their way, as passionate and "true" as Humphrey's is characteristic of the criticism in this vein. To be sure, it follows from Humphrey's jealous refusal to countenance competition that his own attraction to Larsen is more in evidence than Maud's. Nonetheless, the uniform readiness, exemplified in Forrey's analysis, to acquiesce in Humphrey's two-dimensional characterization of Maud may well be the symptom of a cultural squeamishness on the score of sexual desire in women. We have been complicit, perhaps, in the novel's misconstructions. Cultural factors notwithstanding, however, the primary causes of critical shortsightedness in the case of Maud Brewster have been the unconscious distortions and suppressions in the narrative itself.[13]

3

It remains to limn out as plausible and full a portrait of Maud Brewster as the scattered hints and clues in the narrative of *The Sea-Wolf* will permit. The most promising point of departure for this process of reconstruction is to probe more deeply into Humphrey's representation of Maud's responses to Wolf Larsen. For as events unfold, the gap between Maud's actual feelings and Van Weyden's description of them grows wider and more conspicuous. This is the case, for example, when Humphrey rescues Maud from Larsen's attempted rape. Humphrey reacts with "an overmastering rage" at the offender, though it is not clear whether it is Larsen's sexual threat or his evident sexual attraction for Maud that most arouses his jealous anger. In either case, Humphrey is about to stab the mysteriously faltering captain when Maud intervenes with an appeal for mercy:

> Her arms were around me, her hair was brushing my face. My pulse rushed up in unwonted manner, yet my rage mounted with it. She looked me bravely in the eyes.
> "For my sake," she begged.
> "I would kill him for your sake," I cried, trying to free my arm without hurting her.
> "Hush!" she said, and laid her fingers lightly on my lips. I could have kissed them, had I dared, even then, in my rage, the touch of them was so sweet, so very sweet. "Please, please," she pleaded, and she disarmed me by the words, as I was to discover they would ever disarm me. (176–77)

Maud is undoubtedly grateful for timely assistance, but her behavior nonetheless betrays a deeper solicitude for Larsen than circumstances would seem to warrant. The helpless victim of violent sexual assault, she betrays not a flicker of an impulse to punish her attacker. If Humphrey is puzzled by this response, he does not say so; nor does he pause to reflect upon the fact that Maud's embrace is primarily an expression of concern for her brutal assailant. Instead his consciousness is engulfed in Maud's disarming physical attractions. This is evidence that his swing toward the heterosexual side of the erotic spectrum, as described by Charles N. Watson, is well under way. Meanwhile Maud's apparent concern for Larsen, along with the bold directness of her approach and the deft self-confidence of her physical address, combine to suggest that she has the narrator right where she wants him.

This suggestion becomes even stronger as Humphrey's attraction to Maud continues to grow and as Larsen's physical deterioration enters its final phase. These developments combine to create a situation in which Humphrey's infatuated credulity affords Maud greater freedom to exercise her deep concern for the failing captain. This is the case, for example, at the very end of the novel, when Larsen's body is buried at sea. Humphrey looks on as his companion salutes their quondam oppressor: "'Good-by, Lucifer, proud spirit,' Maud whispered, so low that it was drowned by the shouting of the wind; but I saw the movement of her lips and knew" (255–56). Knew what? we may wonder. Humphrey is able to report Maud's words, and we believe that he gets them straight, but he responds with blank literalness to language and gestures that echo and bristle with suggestion. "Lucifer" is a direct reminder of the occasion when Maud responded most intensely to Larsen's sexual power, and it is indirectly allusive to a much broader tradition of romantic rebellion against civilized constraints. Humphrey, the sensitive man of letters, is apparently unmoved. Nor does he register a reaction to the clear possibility that Maud whispers to Larsen because what she has to say is intimate, private, not to be shared. On the other side, however, our narrator's apparent insensitivity is belied by the fact that he listens attentively, and even resorts to lipreading in order to retrieve Maud's words. And he moves with striking rapidity from the observation that Maud addresses Larsen in *sotto voce* to the conclusion that it is the audible force of the gale that nearly drowns her out. In fact we must imagine that the wind's "shouting" is indirectly the expression of a pole of Humphrey's profoundly ambivalent reaction to the scene he witnesses. On one hand, he cannot turn his eyes away; on the other, he cannot bear to see. And although he is careful to listen, he is unwilling to listen carefully.

Humphrey's ambivalence registers textually in a pattern of ironic ambiguity that comes increasingly to characterize the accounts of his exchanges with Maud. The narrative shows more than it consciously

CHAPTER 3

tells because, for reasons that should now be clear, Maud's gains in confidence and assertiveness are matched by a commensurate decline in Humphrey's willingness to see. Accordingly, when Maud learns that Humphrey is about to take revolvers with him on a visit to the enfeebled Wolf Larsen, she pleads with him not to go. Assuming that she is concerned for his own safety, and not for Larsen's, Humphrey lapses into a fatuous effusion: "The dear and lovely woman! And she was so much the woman, clinging and appealing, sunshine and dew to my manhood, rooting it deeper and sending through it the sap of a new strength." Thus exalted, he assures Maud that there is no danger: "I'll merely peep over the bow and see" (216).

Given his assumption about the nature of Maud's solicitude, it is hardly surprising that Humphrey is a bit disconcerted when, a few days later, she urges him to look in on the ailing captain. Now, in place of what he had so confidently assumed was fear for his own welfare, he sees an unmistakable concern for Larsen in Maud's insistence that "we must do something." Puzzled, resistant to an emergent revelation, Humphrey temporizes with "perhaps." Inwardly he frets, "Where was her solicitude for me . . . for me whom she had been afraid to have merely peep aboard?" (216–17). If Humphrey goes on to reflect that Maud's sense of safety is linked to the fact that this time he is unarmed, and therefore scarcely a threat to Larsen, he does not say so. Instead he retreats to the view that her concern is the outgrowth of natural feminine tenderness and charity for human distress wherever it appears.

This episode provides a clear supplement to our understanding of Maud Brewster. First, it tends to confirm that her attraction to Larsen is a much deeper emotion than Humphrey can bear to acknowledge or express in his narrative. It also lends support to the view that Maud is adept at playing along the margins of Humphrey's credulity, and that she is willing and perfectly able, when it is necessary, to coddle him, and to manipulate his pliant readiness to be deceived. Thus when she sees that her manifest care for Larsen is about to arouse Humphrey's resentment, she invites him to view her in a way that is compatible with his vulnerable masculine self-esteem: "You must go aboard, Humphrey," she insists, but "if you want to laugh at me, you have my consent and forgiveness" (217). Once reassured of his own superiority, and of Maud's laughably "feminine" overconcern for Larsen, Humphrey is restored to docile equanimity. He offers no further protest to Maud's request—"I arose obediently and went down the beach"—and when he returns to report that the captain's "head was all right again," Maud is free to display "obvious relief" and "a more cheerful mood" without stirring jealous misgivings. Maud appears to understand that occasional, well-timed strokes to Humphrey's male vanity render him pliant to her will and acquiescent in the illusion that her concern for Larsen is driven by harmless "feminine" solicitude. At the price of at once fueling and surrendering to her companion's foolish condescension, Maud quickly gains the upper hand. When she is next concerned for Larsen's welfare she has only to adopt a properly anxious posture and Humphrey is putty in her hands. "I could see Maud's solicitude again growing," he reports, "though she timidly,—and even proudly, I think,—forebore a repetition of her request. After all, what censure could be put upon her? She was divinely altruistic, and she was a woman. . . . So I did not wait a second time for Maud to send me. I discovered that we stood in need of condensed milk and marmalade, and announced that I was going aboard" (217–18).

Maud must know that Humphrey's blindness, which she quietly and artfully reinforces, is the leading source of her power over him. It is also the source of abundant humor. For once it has been glimpsed, the gathering irony of Humphrey's condescension to Maud becomes impossible to ignore. As we have seen, when Humphrey first interprets Maud's "Please, please" as a sweetly desperate woman's appeal to his superior masculine authority, he fails utterly, and comically, to recognize the extent of Maud's control. The humor redoubles itself later in the narrative when Humphrey adopts a sternly paternal tone in chiding Maud for her misbehavior:

> She looked penitent. "I'll be good," she said, as a naughty child might say it. "I promise—"
> "To obey as a sailor would obey his captain?"
> "Yes," she answered. "It was stupid of me, I know."
> "Then you must promise something else," I ventured.
> "Readily."
> "That you will not say, 'Please, please,' too often; for when you do you are sure to override my authority."
> She laughed with amused appreciation. She, too, had noticed the power of the repeated 'please.'
> "It is a good word—" I began.

"But I must not overwork it," she broke in.
But she laughed weakly, and her head drooped again. (185)

To imagine that Maud Brewster is even remotely genuine in responding as a "naughty" but ultimately docile child is to ignore completely the energy and authority she displays in other circumstances. For special reasons of his own, Humphrey makes this mistake, and his failure to recognize the strength of the woman before him is the source of humor. But the deeper comedy emerges from the gathering impression, underscored here by the debate over the recurrent "Please, please," that Maud's mastery is so complete that she is now free to indulge a bold chuckle at her companion's bottomless folly. Indeed, her amusement may in fact exceed her formidable powers of self-control. Whatever the case, when Humphrey assumes that Maud's laughter expresses her "amused appreciation" of his penetration, his error is comically symptomatic, for it rests on the smug assurance that he is the source of the humor, not its object. But Maud is not laughing with him, she is laughing at his perfectly transcendent obtuseness. Thus it is prudence and not, as Humphrey imagines, weakness that prompts her to drop her head before laughing a second time; after all, to give vent to her real amusement would betray, and therefore jeopardize, her power.[14]

4

Maud resorts twice more to "Please, please" in having her way with Humphrey, and on both occasions the gambit is successful.[15] A leading element in the humor that continues to accumulate with each repetition of the phrase is Humphrey's evident assurance that he gives in to Maud *only* when she uses these words. In fact, he is in a state of continuous submission to her will. He is perhaps easiest for Maud to manipulate when his towering vanity is in the foreground, blinding him to his equally prodigious foolishness. Control is less easily achieved when it comes to Humphrey's much more complex pretensions as a lover. Maud is confronted with a totally inexperienced and hopelessly bookish suitor whose amorous inclinations are deeply ambivalent and, therefore, halting and uncertain in their emergence and expression. Knowing as she must that her ultimate welfare is perilously dependent on Humphrey's wavering masculine will to survive, she must contrive to stimulate and nourish his erotic illusions without precipitating a challenge to his manhood. To make matters even worse, she must somehow control an overpowering impulse to laugh out loud.

The exact course of Maud's approach to an understanding of Humphrey's sexual nature is not easily charted. There is just the slightest suggestion that this process commences on the day of her arrival aboard the *Ghost*. For as "one of the sailors lifted her into Wolf Larsen's downstretched arms, she looked up into our curious faces and smiled amusedly and sweetly" (124). Perhaps her amusement arises from the perception of something more than simple curiosity in Humphrey's eyes. In any case, for many chapters thereafter, and especially after Larsen begins his decline, the reader is witness to Humphrey's gathering impression that he is sexually drawn to Maud. I use "impression" purposely to suggest—what the text certainly suggests—that Humphrey's sexual promptings may in fact be an overflow of literary energies pretty much confined to his head. For if Humphrey admires Maud's "dear, damp brown hair" as it tumbles over her shoulders, and wants "to kiss it, ripple it through my fingers, to bury my face in it," such plausibly sexual ambitions dissipate immediately and entirely in a prolonged meditation on the nature of love, moving from "physical characteristics" through the "essence of the spirit" to closing philosophical reflections on the proposition that "Jehovah was anthropomorphic because he could address himself to the Jews only in terms of their understanding" (182). In the hands of John Donne, such learned metaphysics might well form the prologue to a witty invitation to bed; in the hands of Humphrey Van Weyden, however, they are the expression of a rapid, breathless retreat.

As time passes, Humphrey appears to persuade himself that the obstacles to his erotic self-expression are in fact civilized injunctions to sublimation. Insisting that "the declaration of my love urged and trembled on my tongue a thousand times," he flatters himself "that by look or sign I gave no advertisement of the love I felt for her." This proud assertion of self-control would be more persuasive if it did not resolve itself in the pronouncement that "we were like good comrades, and we grew better comrades as the days went by" (190). Is the model of male friendship resorted to reluctantly, as a necessary alternative to romantic love, or is it the only avenue of erotic expres-

CHAPTER 3

sion presently open to Humphrey? At the very least, we may be sure that he protests too much about the urgency of his passion, and that the principal issue of his sexuality is a confused, increasingly desperate sense of emotional thwartedness. Perhaps Maud senses her companion's frustrated groping; perhaps she has an intimation of the near panic that impels him to resolve to "take her in my arms and proclaim my love, and, with her in my embrace, to make the desperate struggle and die" (192). But there can be no doubt that she comes gradually to recognize his uncertainty, as it expresses itself in a nervous, jerky vacillation between desire and retreat that would be merely touching and amusing were it not for its occasional veerings toward destruction. This characteristic pattern reveals itself in the sequel to the exhilarating seal hunt, when the return to the cove brings Humphrey to the verge of a romantic declaration:

> "It's just like home-coming," Maud said, as I ran the boat ashore.
> I heard her words with a responsive thrill, it was all so dearly intimate and natural, and I said:
> "It seems as though I have lived this life always. The world of books and bookish folk is very vague, more like a dream memory than an actuality. I surely have hunted and forayed and fought all the days of my life. And you, too, seem a part of it. You are—" I was on the verge of saying, "my woman, my mate," but glibly changed it to—"standing the hardship well."
> But her ear had caught the flaw. She recognized a flight that midmost broke. She gave me a quick look.
> "Not that. You were saying—?"
> "That the American Mrs. Meynell was living the life of a savage and living it quite successfully," I said easily.
> "Oh," was all she replied; but I could have sworn there was a note of disappointment in her voice. (204–5)

Maud's unsuccessful attempt to extract an amorous declaration from Humphrey is prompted, it seems likely, by a cluster of interwoven sentiments. There is undoubtedly pleasure in the exercise of her power to attract and control, and there must be amusement. More vitally, there is a determination to cultivate in Humphrey the energy and optimism requisite for survival. She has witnessed his lapses into despondency; she is skillful at bringing him around. Finally, and especially toward the end of the novel, Maud may begin to respond to

Humphrey with affection. If she does warm to him, however, it is with the amused tenderness that an adult might bring to a well-meaning but hopelessly clumsy boy. This perspective on the relationship has an important initial source in the vagueness and ambivalence that characterize Humphrey's attitude toward Maud. "She was," he says more than once, "the one woman in the world—the one small woman, as I loved to think of her" (198). The decided ambiguity of "small" is nowhere more in evidence than when Maud puckishly describes herself to Humphrey as "only one small woman":

> That phrase, the "one small woman," startled me like an electric shock. It was my own phrase, my pet, secret phrase, my love phrase for her.
> "Where did you get that phrase?" I demanded, with an abruptness that in turn startled her.
> "What phrase?" she asked.
> "One small woman."
> "Is it yours?" she asked.
> "Yes," I answered, "mine. I made it."
> "Then you must have talked in your sleep," she smiled.
> The dancing, tremulous light was in her eyes. Mine, I knew, were speaking beyond the will of my speech. I leaned toward her. Without volition I leaned toward her, as a tree is swayed by the wind. Ah, we were very close together in that moment. But she shook her head, as one might shake off sleep or a dream, saying:
> "I have known it all my life. It was my father's name for my mother."
> "It is my phrase, too," I said stubbornly.
> "For your mother?"
> "No," I answered, and she questioned no further, though I could have sworn her eyes retained for some time a mocking, teasing expression. (249–50)

Humphrey's final, rather coy refusal to explain himself does nothing to obscure the fact that Maud is in total control of both the terms and the direction of the conversation. Indeed, it is at once the foundation and the capstone of her authority that her companion is only dimly and fitfully aware that he has been mastered. She has fully fathomed poor Humphrey's "love phrase," and she is positively feline in forcing him to the indirect admission that the words are important to him principally because they are his, and not because they describe her. Having exposed his wonderfully obtuse possessiveness,

CHAPTER 3

Maud then brings attention indirectly to bear on the fact that it is mother, and not a lover, that "one small woman" ultimately points to. Humphrey is perfectly blind to the clear direction of Maud's ironic thrusts, and so he fails to recognize that "The dancing, tremulous light . . . in her eyes" is laughter, and not, as he imagines, amorous excitement. Only at the very end of the encounter does he glimpse her "mocking, teasing expression," but the hint is quickly absorbed, as Maud knows it will be, into Humphrey's infatuated illusions.

This wonderfully funny exchange brings us as close as we come in *The Sea-Wolf* to a direct disclosure of Maud's control of Humphrey's feelings and actions. Her refusal to reveal her mastery is, of course, perfectly apposite: to give up the secret would spoil the fun; and, more crucially, it would totally undermine her control and thereby jeopardize her chances of survival. But the passage is also evidence that Maud gives indirect expression to her hidden feelings with her eyes. The eyes are safer than words, she seems to understand, because their language is so readily misconstrued. Thus the mirth in her glance is lost on Humphrey, who is correct only in assuming that his own eyes "were speaking beyond the will of my speech." Humphrey makes an identical observation earlier in the novel when, after an especially animated discussion with Maud, he wonders whether "our eyes were speaking beyond the will of our speech" (228). The answer to his reiterated concern is evidently affirmative, though it should be added that Maud controls her eyes quite as carefully as she controls her words, and that Humphrey is as tone deaf when it comes to eye speech as he is with the ordinary variety.

I count fifty-six references to eyes in *The Sea-Wolf*, undoubtedly shy a dozen or so from the total. Many of these references are routine descriptions, in themselves hardly noteworthy. But it is notable that the eyes of the novel's principal actors are frequently avenues of expression for powerful emotions, such as the mute "terror" that Humphrey detects in Maud, or the sexual feelings of Wolf Larsen—feelings whose verbal expression would have offended readers of London's time. When the captain is aroused in Maud's presence, "his eyes flash golden" (164). Soon afterward, as he listens to her recital of poetry, his eyes once again flash "their golden light" (174). This pattern culminates when Larsen gives voice to Satan's speech of heroic defiance from *Paradise Lost*. As Larsen speaks, Humphrey observes "his eyes, golden and masculine, intensely masculine and insistently soft, flashing upon Maud at the door" (175).

Rather later in the novel, after the onset of Larsen's physical decline, the initiative in the language of the eyes passes to Maud. Her eyes speak quite directly to Humphrey at the commencement of his protracted struggle to raise the masts on the beached wreck of the *Ghost*. The humor of the situation is aptly characterized by Watson as a "sexual *pas de deux* in which Humphrey struggles to erect the phallic mast on the derelict ship only to have Wolf repeatedly knock it down again."[16] As a first step in the project, Humphrey succeeds in building a pair of "shears," an apparatus designed to lift the heavy masts. Success so excites him that he finds himself "wild with desire, like a child with a new toy, to hoist something with my shears":

> "I wish it weren't so late," I said. "I'd like to see how it works."
> "Don't be a glutton, Humphrey," Maud chided me. "Remember, tomorrow is coming, and you're so tired now that you can hardly stand."
> "And you?" I said, with sudden solicitude. "You must be very tired. You have worked hard and nobly. I am proud of you, Maud."
> "Not half so proud as I am of you, nor with half the reason," she answered, looking me straight in the eyes for a moment with an expression in her own and a dancing, tremulous light which I had not seen before and which gave me a pang of quick delight,—I know not why, for I did not understand it. Then she dropped her eyes, to lift them again, laughing.
> "If our friends could see us now," she said. (228)

Maud cannot fail to be amused by Humphrey's boyish enthusiasm, though her familiar language ("glutton") suggests that her good humor is shaded with impatience. Humphrey responds with praise for her exertions, but his tone is so patronizing, and his judgments so heavily baited for a complimentary response, that Maud's sense of irony seems to ignite. Her reply is perfectly ambiguous, and Humphrey is left trying to make sense of the "dancing, tremulous light" in her eyes. In the upshot, he allows that he is confused, and perhaps he is; but there can be no confusion about the fact that when Maud looks up she is laughing.

We are witness to "the dancing, tremulous light" in Maud's eyes on two occasions, and the aggregate impression yielded by the paired

CHAPTER 3

passages is of warmth arising more out of mirth than out of esteem or affection. A much more somber humor passes through Maud's eyes the third time they light up. The setting is one of gathering desperation. Maud and Humphrey have exhausted themselves in an effort to tow the drifting masts back to their beach. Disheartened, totally fatigued, and apparently resigned to the worst, Humphrey begins to cast off the heavy timbers. Maud can barely contain her panic as she seizes his hand and tries to impress him with the dire consequences of giving up. Humphrey hesitates, but remains undecided until Maud reminds him that towing the mast was his idea: "I want to see you succeed," she urges. He begins to bend under the gratifying weight of her flattery, and Maud, sensing an opportune moment, plays her trump. "I am afraid you will cast off the masts in spite of me," she cries. "Oh, please, please, Humphrey, don't!" The magic words work, the towing continues, a fair wind greets them in the morning, and the newly hopeful Humphrey rouses the hollow-eyed Maud:

> "Oh, you brave, brave woman," I said, when I saw the life coming back into her face. "Did you know that you were brave?"
>
> "I never used to be," she answered. "I was never brave till I knew you. It is you who have made me brave."
>
> "Nor I, until I knew you," I answered.
>
> She gave me a quick look, and again I caught that dancing, tremulous light and something more in her eyes. But it was only for the moment. Then she smiled.
>
> "It must have been the conditions," she said; but I knew she was wrong, and I wondered if she likewise knew. (233–34)

Humphrey may need to feel that Maud is wrong about the "conditions," for the implication of her comment is mordantly ironic. As usual, his tone in this exchange is patronizing and implicitly self-congratulatory. Maud leaves the assertion of her bravery nominally intact, but the insistence that her own virtue merely reflects Humphrey's draws attention to the fact that bravery had virtually nothing to do with the decision to continue with the towing. That decision commences in desperation, passes through panic and fear and transparent flattery, and terminates in a well-timed assertion of power. Thus when Humphrey seizes on Maud's response to claim bravery for himself, the conspicuous lack of precisely that quality falls painfully open to view. Maud may perceive as well that the brief dialogue, ostensibly originating in praise for her, has only begun to serve Humphrey's purposes when the praise, specious and contrived as it is, comes back to shore up his fractured self-esteem. But the truth about bravery would just as surely crush Humphrey now as the weight of failure crushes his spirits the night before. Thus Maud serves the interests of her own survival when she flatters him, and coddles his illusions, and merely hints at what she knows—that it was "conditions," and not bravery, especially not Humphrey's, that got them through. Meanwhile her eyes speak her darkly ironic amusement in terms that her companion cannot possibly fathom.

5

The Maud Brewster who emerges from this analysis is hardly the repressed Victorian prude to be found in most of the criticism of the novel. Rather, she is mature, resourceful, emotionally responsive, shrewd in her assessment and control of her environment, possessed of great good humor, and determined to survive. In all, she is easily the most impressive human being to set foot on the *Ghost*. The men in her world seem hopelessly narrow, obsessive, self-deceived, self-destructive, solipsistic, and, therefore, in one way or another, doomed. It remains to add that this general perspective on the characters in *The Sea-Wolf* raises as many questions as it answers. How, for all these years, can we have been so wide of the mark? If the critics have in fact missed the novel's thrust, especially when it comes to Maud, then why is this so? What is it in our culture, or, more narrowly, in our critical prepossessions, that so blinds us? And what is the relationship between the Maud Brewster who surfaces in this analysis and the intentions of her maker?

It is quite striking, I think, that the critical consensus on the "repressed" Maud Brewster is itself the product of a failure to see, or to fully grasp, what the text makes perfectly clear. Readers since the time of the novel's publication have been readily acquiescent in Humphrey's myopic perspective on Maud. They have been inclined to regard her as an intrusively feminine presence in a bracing, all-male environment. In fact, however, Maud is a challenge in their own terms to the men on board the *Ghost*. She is more resourceful, more adaptable, more capably in control of her surroundings, more likely to survive than any of the men in her midst. Thus Maud is repressed primarily because her audience has repressed her. She is a "twittering" female largely because we have preferred to have her that way. In effect Maud flies in the face of deeply entrenched cultural prepossessions. The persistent failure among readers to fully grasp her character betrays a broadly based resistance to the elements of quiet initiative and self-reliance that emerge in her behavior. We expect women to be passive and dependent, most especially perhaps in the company of strong men.

And yet, of course, the men on the *Ghost* are not strong. Wolf Larsen is a study in the pathology of conventional notions about male strength. He is a Titan brought down by pride, a feeble, impotent superman, inwardly consumed. Maud is undoubtedly drawn to the captain's waning power; more significantly, she seems to gain strength as his drains away. Implicitly, and at times almost overtly, Maud is a challenge to received assumptions about male strength and female weakness. She survives where Larsen succumbs; she takes command from the fatuous, floundering Humphrey. Blindness to Maud's resourcefulness thus figures as a kind of stay against the acknowledgment of depleted male power and authority. The irony of the consensus response to Maud is the more pointed for the fact that it has arisen out of uncritical acquiescence in Humphrey's manifestly homoerotic suppressions.

It is highly unlikely that Jack London set out in *The Sea-Wolf* to offer an analysis and critique of the dominant sexual assumptions of his day. More probably, he identified imaginatively with the doomed rebel at the helm of the *Ghost*—London liked to refer to himself as "Wolf"—and conceived of Maud and Humphrey as the rightful admirers and pale survivors of Larsen's tragic grandeur. Maud's quiet assertiveness and ascendency must figure in this reading as an inadvertent feature of London's design. Modeled as she is on a prominent sexual stereotype, Maud is formed and propelled at least as much by the culture as she is by London. Her complex characterization is evidence that received ideas about "twittering" females were in tension with anxious but unacknowledged intimations about the challenge of the "weaker" sex to male hegemony. London's biography, with its prominent mixtures of male posturing and submerged sexual anxiety, suggests that he was alive in a very personal though largely unconscious way to this dimension in the culture of his time.[17] But the expression of such tensions in numerous of his extremely popular novels and stories indicates in turn that the novelist spoke for a multitude of Americans on this score.

The current revival of interest in London is in part a reassessment of his work as it sheds light on issues of this kind. Kevin Starr's influence has been especially valuable in this regard, as a model for the analysis of London as a kind of cultural barometer.[18] Thanks to Starr, we are more than ever inclined to study the novelist as a window on his times. Yet we are probably not as comfortably detached from London's cultural frames of reference as we would like to think. This is perhaps most especially the case, as *The Sea-Wolf* serves to suggest, in the matter of sexual stereotyping. After all, the virtually unanimous consensus about Maud arises out of a telling blindness to the obvious. For all of our critical sophistication, we have not yet taken control of the cultural reflex at work in Ambrose Bierce's "overwhelming contempt" for the intrusive Miss Brewster.

I will give more attention to the cultural dynamics of such apparently short-sighted reader responses in my final chapter. For now, let me reiterate that *The Sea-Wolf* invites and generously repays much closer textual scrutiny than it has generally received. Consider the novel's conclusion. Viewed in the light of the foregoing analysis, is it possible to accept the virtually unanimous critical view that it is a flat, sentimental, utterly conventional romantic egress? Or is it necessary to entertain the more interesting possibility that this concluding passage is in fact bright and sparkling with irony and humorous suggestion?

"We are saved," I said soberly and solemnly. And then, in an exuberance of joy, "I hardly know whether to be glad or not."

I looked at her. Our eyes were not loath to meet. We leaned toward each other, and before I knew it my arms were about her.

"Need I?" I asked.

And she answered, "There is no need, though the telling of it would be sweet, so sweet."

Her lips met the press of mine, and by what strange trick of the imagination I know not, the scene in the cabin of the *Ghost* flashed

CHAPTER 3

upon me, when she had pressed her fingers lightly on my lips and said, "Hush, hush."

"My woman, my one small woman," I said, my free hand petting her shoulder in the way all lovers know though never learn in school.

"My man," she said, looking at me for an instant with tremulous lids which fluttered down and veiled her eyes as she snuggled her head against my breast with a happy little sigh.

I looked toward the cutter. It was very close. A boat was being lowered.

"One kiss, dear love," I whispered. "One kiss more before they come."

"And rescue us from ourselves," she completed, with a most adorable smile, whimsical as I had never seen it, for it was whimsical with love. (29)

What shall we make of Humphrey's mingled response to the rescue, and of his final refusal (or incapacity) to find words for his feelings? By what "strange trick of the imagination" does his consciousness leap from this, their first embrace, to Maud's earlier, enigmatic defense of the sexually threatening Wolf Larsen? What, specifically, does this lapse suggest about the depth of Humphrey's confidence in Maud's esteem and in his own readiness for this passionate, heterosexual attachment? On the other side, when Maud drops her eyes and sighs, is she surrendering to love, as Humphrey would have it, or is she suppressing a rather different response to her companion's "pet phrase"? Finally—though this hardly exhausts the questions the passage gives rise to—is Maud as "adorable" and "whimsical" as Humphrey imagines, or is her concluding statement expressive of sentiments characteristically complex, ironic, and utterly remote from the comprehension of her interlocutor?

4

SHANE

1

The title character of Jack Schaefer's classic, *Shane*, may be said to embody virtually all of the qualities usually associated with the Western hero—or, indeed, more generally with the American hero. He is handsome, youthful, even boyish. Joe Starrett, the proud homesteader who befriends Shane, remarks to the gunfighter, "There's still a lot of kid in you." Young Bob Starrett, Joe's son and only child, goes on: "The first real smile I had seen yet flashed across Shane's face. 'Maybe. Maybe there is at that.'"[1] He is utterly independent and self-reliant—"cool and competent," Bob observes, at a climactic moment, "facing that room full of men in the simple solitude of his own invincible completeness" (254). He is "as self-sufficient as the mountains" (161). And when the chips are down, he reminds Bob's father, "There's no man living can tell me what I can't do. Not even you, Joe" (243). He is solitary, taciturn, socially remote. "Shane was not anxious to meet people. He would share little in their talk" (124). He has no respect for the other homesteaders, and he makes no effort to disguise his contempt (165). He is itinerant and homeless—"I was fiddle-footed and left home at fifteen" (77), he declares—and disinclined to talk at any length about his past. "He had no news about himself," says Bob. "His past was fenced as tightly as our pasture" (71). As Bob insists at the novel's end, Shane's origins are mythical, intertwined with the destiny of the region and the nation, and somehow subsumed in the latitude of his autonomy and the depth of his self-completeness. "He was the man who rode into our little valley out of the heart of the

CHAPTER 4

great glowing West and when his work was done rode back whence he had come and he was Shane" (274). "No bullet can kill that man," observes another of the homesteaders; "Sometimes I wonder whether anything ever could" (266).

Shane's autonomy and invincibility are inseparable from his spareness and simplicity. He is uneducated. This apparent lack is in fact a source of strength, for there is no veneer of sophistication to obstruct or obscure his natural, integral authority. "What a man knows isn't important," says Joe. "It's what he is that counts" (119). It is knowledge of farming that Starrett has in mind, but his words point toward the larger futility of "book-learning." Thus Shane is a man of very few words. When he speaks, he does so primarily with actions. He says nothing to Joe about uprooting the enormous stump that stands near the farmhouse. Instead, without so much as a word's warning, he assaults it, and Joe soon joins him in the silent, exhilarating test of strength. The episode advances through two brief, tellingly silent tableaus. As the work begins in earnest, the men's "eyes met over the top of the stump and held and neither of them said a word. Then they swung up their axes and both of them said plenty to that old stump" (93). Much later, when the work is finally done, "they both looked up and their eyes met and held as they had so long ago in the morning hours." Bob goes on: "The silence should have been complete. It was not because someone was shouting, a high-pitched, wordless shout. I realized that the voice was mine and I closed my mouth. The silence was clean and wholesome, and this was one of the things you could never forget whatever time might do to you in the furrowing of the years, an old stump on its side with root ends making a strange pattern against the glow of the sun sinking behind the far mountains and two men looking over it into each other's eyes." (107–8).

The wordless communication between the two men is a stage in the deep moral and emotional bonding between them. It is rooted in the mutual possession and recognition of the qualities that I have drawn into association with Shane's heroism, and it expresses itself in the readiness, even eagerness, to make the ultimate sacrifice. Bob is quite literally transported by this rare spectacle of male intimacy; it imprints itself in his consciousness as the deepest and most authentic of human connections, a model for life. In its wake, and as if to confirm his profound first impressions, he is struck with evidence of change in Shane: "It scarce seemed possible that he was the same man I had first seen, stern and chilling in his dark solitude, riding up our road. Something in father, something not of words or of actions but of the essential substance of the human spirit, had reached out and spoken to him and he had replied to it and had unlocked a part of himself to us" (113–14). The powerful homoerotic dimension to the relationship between Shane and Joe, who exchange long, knowing, silent glances across the base of the stump, is perfectly manifest. This, clearly, is the supreme expression of human love—this "clean and wholesome," wordless intercourse between two men. The utter silence is offered as an index to the strength of the bonds that tie Shane and Joe. These are feelings too profoundly good for mere words. By contrast, the shallowness and inauthenticity of male/female relations in the novel are made quite as manifest by their dependence on language. The leading offender in this regard is Marian, who is cast as the hopelessly weak member in the novel's erotic triangle. Words give expression to what is represented as frivolous and ephemeral in her nature, but they are also the agents of her sexual vanity and manipulativeness. Thus as Joe and Shane labor silently over the great stump, she dresses herself in her prettiest clothes and advances toward the men, feeling "mighty proud of herself." They are "so busy and intent that even if they were aware she was there they did not really notice her." Finally, at her insistence, they pause and offer perfunctory praise. But then Joe speaks his mind: "'Now stop bothering us. Can't you see we're busy?' And he swung back to his root" (95–96).

Evidently threatened by the obvious intimacy between the workers, and by the failure of her charms to break the spell, Marian retreats to a second line of defense—food. But again she is frustrated, not merely because her cooking fails to displace the work as the center of energy and attention but also because in her own fascination with the epic labor she forgets her pie, and it is ruined. "'Oh-h-h—you—you—men!'" she cries out. "'You made me forget about it! It's probably all burned!' And she was running for the house so fast she was tripping over her skirt." Marian recoils bravely from this descent to failure and ridicule by laboring at length, and with fierce independence, over a new pie. It's "prime," too, as Shane readily acknowledges. "Yes," he goes on, "that's the best bit of stump I ever tasted" (108–11). But Marian's triumph is a slender one, for it is conferred in a tone of jocular condescension that bears with it the clear implication that her success issues directly from the subordination of her "feminine" qualities to the kinds of "male" virtue that go into subduing the stump.

The irony at Marian's expense is deeper for the fact that she is distracted from her own work by the much more fascinating spectacle of the men at theirs. She is fixed, as the much larger audience is fixed, by the exhibition of male strength in vigorous action. This magnetic core to the novel's attraction finds its center in Shane, and its consummate expression in his periodic eruptions into massive violence. "Magnificient" is the word that Marian settles on to describe the exploits of Joe and Shane in their bloody triumph at Grafton's Saloon (201). Such eruptions of violence are the business of men; and among men, Shane is unique for the explosive force of the energy concentrated inside him. He is a kind of bomb, and his audience looks on in awe of his power, and in anticipation of its inevitable display. As he makes his final assault on the stump, Shane's eyes "were aflame with a concentrated cold fire. Not another separate discernible movement did he make. It was all of him, the whole man, pulsing in the one incredible surge of power. You could fairly feel the fierce energy suddenly burning in him, pouring through him in the single coordinated drive" (106–7).

Much later, after he has "exploded into action" in Grafton's Saloon, Shane pauses to vent his delight in battle: "He was standing there, straight and superb, the blood on his face bright like a badge, and he was laughing. It was a soft laugh, soft and gentle, not in amusement at Red Marlin or any single thing, but in the joy of being alive and released from long discipline and answering the urge in mind and body. The lithe power in him, so different from father's sheer strength, was singing in every fiber of him" (191–92). Here we are witness to the essential Shane, the man for whom it is natural and therefore desirable to break free of all restraints into an exuberant display of awesome physical power. This release "from long discipline" is the source of enormous pleasure to Shane, as it is, quite as obviously, to Bob, and to most others in the audience. The "singing" of this "lithe power" is what we came to hear.

But it is a spectacle that may stir rather mixed feelings. All of the Starretts recognize that Shane is a dangerous man; not surprisingly, therefore, they are grateful that he is also a friend. Bob is quite understandably impressed with the "indescribable deadliness" (88) that he witnesses in the singular stranger. It is Shane himself, however, his relish for violence notwithstanding, who has the deepest misgivings about this most natural of his inclinations. He is regularly stirred to sadness by memories of bloodshed "along the dark trail of the past" (139). His stunning victory over the villainous Stark Wilson has its strange sequel in depression: "'I gave him his chance,' he murmured out of the depths of a great sadness" (258). It is Bob's impression that Shane is "hurt" to find that the Starretts have been spectators to his victory at Grafton's (196). "A woman shouldn't have to see things like that" (201), he instructs Marian. And when Shane backs away from a fight with a cowboy named Chris, one astute observer assures the others: "He wasn't afraid of Chris. He was afraid of himself" (157).

Shane is deeply divided. His pleasure in violence is countered by sadness and shame; his predatory instinct is in tension with an aversion to the consequences of struggle. Shane gives signs of an awareness of the contradiction within himself, and takes the view that it is rooted in the fixed foundation of his makeup. "A man is what he is, Bob, and there's no breaking the mold." Shane goes on to add that his brief sojourn as a farmer has been a losing effort to break out of old patterns. But, he observes, it was a mistake that sprang from his initial, very positive response to Bob ("a freckled kid on a rail up the road") and the desire to help "back him for the chance another kid never had" (263). Put another way, Shane's identification with young Bob Starrett inspires him to try to steer the boy away from the life of a gunfighter. He cannot break his own mold, but he labors heroically to insure that Bob is formed from a different one. He does this by giving his support to the Starrett family, the boy's best hope for a life free of rootlessness and bloodshed. Ironically, in giving his support Shane is obliged to endure precisely that violence and uprootedness that he hopes to spare Bob. He suffers that the boy may have a home. "It's up to you now," he counsels young Starrett. "Go home to your mother and father. Grow strong and straight and take care of them." Recognizing the hard truth that "there's only one thing more I can do" (263) for the family, he leaves the valley forever, bearing the wounds and the stigma of violence with him.

2

The spirit manifest in Shane's great sacrifice remains in the valley, and serves to bind the Starretts to their home. "He's here, in this place, in this place he gave us," Marian proclaims. "We have roots here now that we can never tear loose" (270–71). Of course, her words of triumph illustrate that the deep tension in Shane between the natural urge and the reluctance to engage in violence has a correlative in the contradiction between the values that attach to his heroism and the values that inspire him to support the Starretts. In taking his stand for the family, the gunfighter brings his heroic qualities to the service of home and hearth, continuity, the community and its array of social, educational, legal, and other institutions: to all that is Eastern and European and civilized. To all, in short, that he is not. We may be tempted to respond that the Starretts are a special family and represent a new, Western American alternative to the old, fallen order of things. This may be the promise that Shane responds to when he first casts his eye on what Bob calls "our place." It was "not much," he says, "if you were thinking in terms of size and scope. But what there was was good. You could trust father for that. The corral, big enough for about thirty head if you crowded them in, was railed right to true sunk poles. The pasture behind, taking in nearly half of our claim, was fenced tight. The barn was small, but it was solid, and we were raising a loft at one end for the alfalfa growing green in the north forty. We had a fair-sized field in potatoes that year and father was trying a new corn he had sent all the way to Washington for and they were showing properly in weedless rows" (64). "Good," "railed right," "true sunk poles," "fenced tight," "growing green in the north forty," "weedless rows"—this is the vocabulary of an immemorial American dream of yeoman prosperity in the Garden of the New World. But how does this idyllic image compare with the larger picture of domesticity that emerges from the novel as a whole?

"You could trust father" to make things "good," Bob feels sure, but he does not make the same claim for his mother. Indeed, viewed closely, Bob's narrative complicates the portrait of the good mate and mother with hints that Marian is deeply self-interested and subtly manipulative. In all of this, her sexuality is her most potent weapon, and her most damning flaw. This is especially the case, we are led to suppose, when there is "a real man" around. "She was an unpredictable woman" (70), Bob reflects, when his mother betrays a special responsiveness to the handsome stranger. In fact Marian's behavior around the gunfighter is increasingly predictable. When the center of attention turns to stumps, and the male bonds begin to tighten, Marian asserts herself sexually, as if to obstruct the obvious drift of things. Vanity and jealousy are doubtlessly at work here, but before long it becomes clear that Marian's assertiveness is more generally in the service of her determination to build and preserve a home. She is the first to observe the heavy personal price that Shane pays for his involvement in the fight to protect their homesteader's claim. She blames Joe, confronting him with "what you've done to Shane" (171). But rather than act on her insight to relieve the gunfighter, she makes her own direct and very artful appeal for his support. She calls Shane to the house and explains, "I've been wanting to talk to you when Joe wasn't around." Shane is obviously stirred by this opening gambit: he calls her "Marian," and Bob observes "a tenderness in his eyes he had for no one else." Marian acknowledges her awareness that Shane is worried "about what may happen in this Fletcher business," and "about what [he] might do if there's any more fighting." He replies:

> "You're a discerning woman, Marian."
> "You've been worrying about something else too."
> "You're a mighty discerning woman, Marian."
> "And you've been thinking that maybe you'll be moving on."
> "And how did you know that?"
> "Because it's what you ought to do. For your own sake. But I'm asking you not to." Mother was intense and serious, as lovely there with the light striking through her hair as I had ever seen her. "Don't go, Shane. Joe needs you. More than ever now. More than he would ever say."
> "And you?" Shane's lips barely moved and I was not sure of the words.
> Mother hesitated. Then her head went up. "Yes. It's only fair to say it. I need you too."
> "So-o-o," he said softly, the words lingering on his lips. He considered her gravely. "Do you know what you're asking, Marian?"

CHAPTER 4

"I know. And I know that you're the man to stand up to it. In some ways it would be easier for me, too, if you rode out of this valley and never came back. But we can't let Joe down. I'm counting on you not ever to make me do that. Because you've got to stay, Shane, no matter how hard it is for us. Joe can't keep this place without you. He can't buck Fletcher alone" (175–77).

The line separating self-interest from self-sacrifice in Marian's appeal is of course very difficult to locate. But it is apparent, I think, that she draws attention to Joe's absence and to the "something else" between her and Shane as ways of bending the gunfighter to her purposes. Only then, when this hint of intimacy has been ventured, does she appeal to Shane in her husband's behalf, because "Joe needs you." Shane brings her back to an acknowledgment of *her* interest in the matter, and to the magnitude of *her* request. She responds by acknowledging a personal interest in Shane, though in a way that construes his sacrifice as in some measure her own. Thus she insists, "*we* can't let Joe down." Shane withdraws into silence. "It seemed to me," Bob says, "that he was troubled and hard pressed in his mind." Apparently sensing a similar uncertainty, Marian redoubles her efforts at persuasion. And again, though her appeal is advanced in Joe's name and in Joe's interests, her personal ambitions seem to provide much of the energy and direction in what she has to say. "It would just about kill Joe to lose this place. He's too old to start in again somewhere else," she observes, and "he promised me this place when we were married." It's home, and "nothing else would ever be the same."

Shane's response does nothing to diminish the almost palpable strain in the exchange, the pervasive mood of doubleness and doubt. He

> drew a deep breath and let it ease out slowly. He smiled at her and yet, somehow, as I watched him, my heart ached for him. "Joe should be proud of a wife like you. Don't fret any more, Marian. You'll not lose this place."
> Mother dropped back in her chair. Her face, the side I could see from the window, was radiant. Then, woman like, she was talking against herself. "But that Fletcher is a mean and tricky man. Are you sure it will work out all right?"
> Shane was already starting toward the barn. He stopped and turned

to look at her again. "I said you won't lose this place." You knew he was right because of the way he said it and because he said it. (177–178)

Bob is dimly alive to something of constraint and reluctance in Shane's mood. His use of "fret" to characterize Marian's appeal suggests that it is not her right-mindedness that he has surrendered to. And the "you" in "you'll" is inherently ambiguous. Bob is even less aware of the range of meanings that may attach to his mother's behavior. Is she "radiant" on Joe's account? or because she has had her own way, and because she has had it with Shane? Bob recognizes that her remarks about Fletcher seem inconsistent ("woman like"), but he may not see that they cost her little, knowing as she does (and as her radiance suggests) that Shane is where she wants him. Thus her concessions and expression of concern are primarily self-appeasing— they allow her the illusion that such sentiments have figured prominently in her approach to the matter. Shane, I think, is not impressed. To the contrary, he repeats himself in a way that suggests an impatience with Marian's inauthenticity. Your concern for me comes too late, he seems to say; but don't worry, I (at least) mean what I say. Once again, Bob puts a positive face on things. Yet his narrative conveys the strong suggestion that Shane has been seduced, and knows it.

To be sure, this exchange between Shane and Marian is extremely ambiguous. Indeed, in itself the passage is so elusive that it hardly permits a confidently singular line of analysis. This is to acknowledge that my understanding of this interval in the novel is influenced by developments at other points in the narrative. For example, the reading here developed seems to find confirmation in Marian's behavior later on in the story, when Joe decides, against what appear to be impossible odds, to continue the struggle against Fletcher. "There are some things a man can't take," he insists. "Not if he's to go on living with himself." In response, Shane struggles inwardly with "that old hidden desperation"; he recoils from the prospect of more bloodshed, but he is also moved by Joe's courage, and bound to him by deep friendship. After a brief pause, but quite without a word, he heads for the barn, evidently ready to fight at Joe's side. Joe responds by admitting that Shane's support is indispensable to their cause ("my weight in any kind of a scale won't match his and I know it"). But he is also more alert than ever to the heavy price that Shane is paying for

CHAPTER 4

their friendship. Had he been aware of this from the beginning, Joe insists, "I'd never have got him to stay on here." In the upshot, he is unwilling to allow Shane to sacrifice himself further. "Fletcher can have his way. We'll sell out and move on."

Without stopping to think, Bob reacts: "Father! Shane wouldn't run away." Marian agrees. "Bob's right, Joe. We can't let Shane down." Earlier, it was Shane's duty to support Joe. Now, according to Marian, it is Joe's duty to support Shane. Bob pauses to acknowledge a vague uneasiness about his mother's intentions. "It was queer," he says, "hearing her say the same thing to father she had said to Shane, the same thing with only the name different." What he seems poised to recognize is the implausibility of his mother's claim, and, further, the extent to which that implausibility draws her unacknowledged self-interest into focus. Shane is obviously reluctant to risk more bloodshed, and Joe is persuaded that it is unfair to permit more sacrifice. Frustrated in her own ambitions by this turn of events, Marian draws Joe's attention away from Shane's suffering and obvious reluctance and emphasizes instead the "something bigger" that ties the family to the land, the shame of "running away," and the fact that in the wake of failure "there wouldn't be anything real ahead of us, any of us, maybe even for Bob, all the rest of our lives." In fact, this is more warning than encouragement; Marian defines the sequel to failure in terms that feature her own disapproval of Joe's performance as husband and father. So confronted, Joe loses sight of Shane altogether, and acquiesces in Marian's vague optimism that "this will work out some way." She will not say as much, but her confidence is rooted in the assurance of Shane's support. Joe joins the happy round of self-deception. Yes, he agrees, "maybe we can wait Fletcher out and make him overplay his hand. The town won't take much to this Wilson deal. Men like that fellow Weir have minds of their own" (221–25). This is all the flimsiest brand of rationalization, and deep down Joe must know it. Simply put, his decision to continue to fight Fletcher is a decision to accept Shane's agonized offer of assistance. He is quite as unwilling as Marian to acknowledge this. Perhaps he accepts her invitation to view their position as a favor to Shane. In fact, however, Marian's appeal to Joe's ambitions, and her implied challenge to his male pride, are the levers that turn him away from Shane, and from Shane's claims on his careful concern.

3

Whatever his intentions may have been, Jack Schaefer gave life in *Shane* to an extremely subtle and complicated triangular struggle.[2] There is undoubtedly some truth to Marian's claim that Shane expects the Starretts to dig in and fight Fletcher; he will respect that decision, she knows, and he will support it. She knows, too, that he is personally drawn to her, just as she knows that he is not a man to run from trouble. Moreover, she is understandably jealous of the deep love that has sprung up between the gunfighter and her husband. Joe's readiness to honor Shane's feelings speaks eloquently of that bond, and we can well understand her impulse to subvert it, to displace Shane's claims on Joe with her own. But above all else, she is determined to have the farm. It is, as the novel amply demonstrates, the arena in which her activities are most highly valued, and in which she exercises the maximum personal power. It is the place, in other words, where she can most effectively compete with the men for authority and self-esteem. She is ready, I think, to subordinate virtually all other human claims to this one. She would rather risk Joe's life in the struggle with Fletcher than face the prospect of losing the homestead. She is obviously quite ready to use Shane in the service of the same end. And she is subtly and shrewdly adept at maneuvering the men into line with her objectives.

Marian's determination to achieve something like parity in matters of power and self-respect are hardly unreasonable. Although we may find fault with her methods, we may also be forced to grant that she has few if any effective alternatives. Moreover, her strong impulse to use Shane is in tension with genuine desire for him, and her desire, potent with harm, is in turn a source of confusion and fear. Much of this tangling in her makeup and intentions comes to view just after the fight at Grafton's Saloon. In spite of Shane's evident discomfort at her having witnessed the struggle, Marian insists on a thorough review of the action. "You were magnificent," she tells him. "You were so cool and quick and—and dangerous and—." She assures him that she does not judge him for his descent to violence. "You didn't start it. You didn't want to do it. Not until they made you anyway. You did it because you had to." As she continues to speak, Marian grows more and more excited. "Her voice was climbing," Bob observes,

CHAPTER 4

"and she was looking back and forth and losing control of herself. 'Did ever a woman have two such men?' And she turned from them and reached out blindly for a chair and sank into it and dropped her face into her hands and the tears came" (201–2).

Marian's breathless fascination with Shane's fighting qualities is so heavily charged with erotic energy that her subsequent moral commentary seems pale and perfunctory. She is flattered and stimulated by the physical display, and we may suspect that her defense of Shane's motives is primarily intended to ease his conscience and sense of shame, and thereby to bolster his wavering commitment to the struggle. Her insistence that Shane fought because he "had to" may give us pause, for the imperative in the matter was not morality but Marian herself. Shane had to fight because Marian insisted upon it, and she insisted, I have argued, because of her determination to keep the farm. The ulterior motive is here found in strained combination with desire, and both are submerged in a flimsy, self-serving appeal to moral necessity. No wonder Marian comes to tears. As the precariously accelerating pace of her remarks suggests, the tangle of impulse and implication in her having "two such men" is at least temporarily more than she can bear.

Shane quickly withdraws, and Joe steps out onto the porch while Marian composes herself. After a short while, she calls Joe in. "She stretched her hands toward him and he was there and had her in his arms. 'But you think I don't know, Marian?'" he says.

> "But you don't. Not really. You can't. Because I don't know myself."
> Father was staring over her head at the kitchen wall, not seeing anything there. "Don't fret yourself, Marian. I'm man enough to know a better when his trail meets mine. Whatever happens will be all right."
> "Oh, Joe . . . Joe! Kiss me. Hold me tight and don't ever let go." (203)

Clearly, Joe recognizes his wife's attraction to Shane, and he sympathizes with it. But Marian rejects his interpretation. We can only guess at what her tentative remarks add up to, but it appears that she is thinking out loud, venturing ideas darkly, in part because she is confused and in part because she wants to deny Joe's suggestion but perceives as she does so that her deeper motives, which Joe cannot possibly glimpse, are even less flattering to both of them. Thus she denies his reading of the situation, but then, for rather different reasons, denies her own as well. Finally she simply buries her head, and all her contrary, unsettling thoughts, in Joe's embrace.

Marian's confusion and final retreat from self-reckoning should not be taken as failures of intelligence or virtue; rather, they are part of the heavy price she pays for her rebellion against "the woman's role" in her social and cultural setting. As I have already indicated, if Marian is to compete successfully for power and self-esteem, then she has scant alternative to the deeply compromising course that she pursues. The more we study her behavior, the more we are compelled to sympathize with her painful confusion, admire her independence, and acknowledge the ample measure of justice in her lonely cause.

The sustained scrutiny of Joe's behavior yields a different result. We are impressed with his responsiveness to Shane's suffering and with his remarkable readiness to sympathize with Marian's attraction to the gunfighter, but we have also observed his insensitivity to Marian's demands for attention and respect and his ready acquiescence in her rationalizations about not letting Shane down. In this light Joe appears no less compromised than his wife. This line of speculation finds considerable support in developments at the homestead just before the final showdown with Fletcher. Once again it is clear, though never stated, that the outcome depends entirely on Shane's participation. And again his inner torment is obvious. When it comes finally to a decision, Shane again overcomes his reluctance and straps on his gun. Joe insists, "It's my stand. Fletcher's making his play against me. There's no dodging. It's my business" (242). Joe's protests come much too late, and, indeed, there is good evidence that he protests too much. For in the moments leading up to Shane's anguished decision, Joe does nothing to dissuade his friend from the course of violence. Rather, he offers Bob what he views as a likely outcome of the conflict. "Fletcher'll be done. The town will see to that. I can't beat Wilson on the draw. But there's strength enough in this clumsy body of mine to keep me on my feet till I get him, too." Significantly, Marian offers no objection to Joe's apparent intentions. "Mother stirred and was still" (238). But Shane moves—as everyone knew he would—toward the barn, where he keeps his gun.

The contradiction between Joe's objective in offering this plangent tableau of mortal self-sacrifice and his subsequent refusal to accept Shane's help is painfully obvious. Its significance becomes even clearer when he addresses his wife, who pursues Shane halfway to

CHAPTER 4

the barn but then, stopping "abruptly at the house corner, clutching at the wood, panting and irresolute," turns slowly back. "I'm counting on you, Marian," Joe says, "to help him win again. You can do it, if anyone can" (239). Not only does Joe here reveal that he has been banking on Shane's help from the start, and that he has manipulated shamelessly to gain it, but he also betrays a readiness to pander with his wife's charms in order to have his way. Marian's silence in the face of her husband's pitiful scenario, and her failure to offer Shane any discouragement, are good indications that she has seen Joe's drift all along and, despite some concern at the prospect of Shane's loss, has seen her way to going along with it. Thus she tacitly assents to her husband's suggestion that she prime Shane for the struggle. In fact, when she is finally alone with the gunfighter, there are indications that she is prepared to discourage him from violence, but only if he concedes that he is prompted to fight solely on her account.

Clearly enough, Joe and Marian operate in silent collaboration to move Shane to their purposes. And while their purposes are different in ways that neither fully perceives, it is safe to say that both are deeply self-interested and consciously deceptive and deftly manipulative in their behavior. In Marian's behalf it must be said that she responds to a powerful urge to intercept Shane on the way to the barn. Granted, she gives up the chase, but she may see the futility of trying to change his mind and not just the advantages of letting him go. But if Marian wavers between contrary impulses to possess Shane and to use him, so does Joe. He is hardly likely to recognize the strong erotic element in his esteem for Shane; to do so he would have to hurdle cultural obstacles at least as high as those that confront Marian. Instead he readily submerges desire and pursues a more or less singular and calculated line of self-interest. In adopting this course, he is certainly no more fair-minded than his wife, and perhaps less honest. He pays for this, as we shall see, in diminished self-esteem and a readiness—bordering on a wish—to die.

4

Thus we are confronted with the paradox that Shane's heroic sacrifices in the service of the all-American family have the effect of undermining that institution by drawing out the weaknesses in the adult members, and by exposing the tensions and moral flaws in their way of living. If it is clearly Shane's intention in all this to anchor Bob in the family, and to insure that he is formed in its wholesome mold, then it is just as surely the impact of his example and activity to frustrate that intention. In helping Joe and Marian, Shane stimulates and exposes their shortcomings; in vigorously advocating the value of the home, he reveals what a shallow and constraining and vulnerable place it is. And all of this ironically inadvertent iconoclasm occurs before the eyes of Bob, who tells the story, and who is thus the primary witness to the developments at the homestead. This is at least the first step toward an explanation for the fact that Bob tells two stories: one, a mingled tale of heroism and utopian domesticity; the other, a subversive undercutting of the first. But how, we may wonder, does all of this disenchantment find its way into his narrative when it finds so little place in what appears to be his conscious intention as a storyteller?

From the beginning young Bob Starrett is almost obsessively concerned to deny that he has any clear understanding of the "adult" actions and implications of his story. The sheer frequency of his disclaimers gives the narrative a strangely furtive quality, a feeling of nervously constrained voyeurism. "I was a kid" (61) when it all happened, he begins, stressing his youth and innocence. Thus in Shane's clothes he detects "a hint of men and manners alien to my limited boy's experience" (63). Later, Bob remembers, there was a "strange wildness" in Shane's eyes "that I could not understand." But he concludes that Shane "was a man like father in whom a boy could believe in the simple knowing that what was beyond comprehension was still clean and solid and right" (90–91). Still, Bob is puzzled by Shane's comment on his mother's pie ("What could a silly remark like that mean?"), and he cannot "straighten out" in his mind "the way the grown folks had behaved, the way things that did not really matter so much had become so important to them" (111–13). This puzzlement at adult behavior has its correlative in bafflement at the "sudden fierce energy" that flares up in Shane, and that takes its rise from "things in the human equation beyond my comprehension" (121–22). Bob cannot fathom the dark mood that overtakes Shane when he thinks on the past (139), and he is unable to make sense of the gunfighter's explanation of the necessity for violence: "What he was trying to explain to me," Bob confesses, "was beyond my comprehension then"

(174). This lurking element of threat in the hero surfaces fully, if enigmatically, as Shane leaves the farm on his way to town for the final shoot-out. At that moment, Bob recalls, "he was the symbol of all the dim, formless imaginings of danger and terror in the untested realm of human potentialities beyond my understanding. The impact of the menace that marked him was like a physical blow" (249).

The pattern that surfaces in this selection of examples is a clear one. Adult behavior is a mystery to Bob. The undercurrent of implication in grown-up gestures and speech does not escape his notice, but it eludes what he refers to again and again as his "comprehension." This wide-eyed innocence is most emphatically underlined at moments when the adults seem most compromised in their dealings with one another. Thus when Marian collapses in tears over "having" two men, Bob looks on as "the two men stared at her and then at each other in that adult knowledge beyond my understanding" (202). Then, after Joe acknowledges that Shane is the "better" man, and Marian surrenders to confusion, Bob reiterates: "What happened in our kitchen that night was beyond me in those days" (204). What must finally baffle the reader in all this rather studied ignorance is why the narrator, the now adult Bob who looks back on his childhood as he tells his tale, is so determined to conceal what he seems to recognize (in the present of the telling) about the past. It may be replied that this simulation of the boy's point of view is requisite to the maintenance of the mythic, heroic, larger-than-life cast of the narrative. But if this is so, why is the narrative so heavily laden with hints and suggestions, arising directly from the boy's point of view, that undermine that mythic tone? No, the management of point of view is subtly subversive of the narrative's heroic trajectory, and this tension, amounting to an outright contradiction, is vital not only to our understanding of Bob, but also to our understanding of his story.

Bob's simulation of a boy's perspective is the reflex of an *adult* refusal to accept the truth of the past. Bob cannot deny that as an adult he understands what as a child he could not comprehend. But he never gets down to declaring in detail what it is that he knows. Rather he sees only to deny that he has seen; he tells only to deny what he has told. Now much of the emergent implication that Bob denies turns up at the center of my analysis of the novel. My reading of *Shane*, in other words, has to this point entailed making explicit what I have called Bob's second story, the array of equivocal implyings and denyings that work to subvert the confident forward motion of his narrative. In order to make better sense of this pattern of denial, however, we must turn to Bob's present motives for telling his story. What prompts him to set out on this narrative whose range of implication, he finds in the telling, he cannot fully accept?

Viewed from this angle, *Shane* is the dramatic record of adult disenchantment as it gives rise to the attempted reconstruction—verging, one suspects, on sheer fabrication—of an enchanted childhood alternative. Bob's leading impulse, the evidence strongly suggests, is to somehow cancel or un-know his adult understanding of experience. Predictably, however, the attempt to nullify adult disenchantment issues in the virtual recapitulation of the original fall from bliss: the heroic/utopian fantasy is everywhere vulnerable to a complete return of the repressed adult perspective. Indeed, the pressure of adult disenchantment is nowhere more manifest than in Bob's persistent denials of comprehension. His refusal to see is the direct manifestation in the simulated boy of the repressive impulse in the presiding adult. The innocent failure of comprehension that Bob insists upon is thus part of his fiction, and of a process of repression that began years ago when the "real" events took place. He has been over this ground before; and he will be back.

Bob Starrett is a man whose notions about innocence and experience strongly incline him to admire a fictional hero like Shane. The hero as he recurs to Bob's memory—"the Shane of the adventures I had dreamed for him" (253–54)—is the disenchanted adult's compromise with reality. We must be struck with the extent to which Bob's words bear with them the acknowledgment that Shane is a fabrication, a fiction. But it never occurs to him that Shane is the answer in fantasy to the disillusioning spectacle of domestic disenchantment submerged in his superficially untroubled portraits of home and mother and dad. This is so in some measure because Shane's actions answer Bob's need in a second way, and at a second level, by filling the foreground of the narrative and thus obscuring the rather messy maneuvering going on in the background. Thus the heroic narrative is instrumental in the repression of those disillusioning insights that it answers at the level of unconscious fantasy. To be sure, Shane has a past, but it is vague in content and heroic at the very least in the edge it lends to his continuing self-sacrifice. He is violent. But the violence is reluctant, slow to erupt, "necessary," just, painful to its heroic agent, and exhilarating for Bob in part because it is rained down in massive quantities by a man-child on the heads of corrupt, corrupting adults. Bob's suppressed rage in his disenchantment expresses itself in Shane's "natural" pleasure, an exuberant liberation from "long discipline" in titanic, vengeful, morally retributive violence.

Finally, and as Marian Starrett recognizes, the violence is "magnificent." Marian is ultimately content to channel Shane's energy into the service of the farm, but not without first responding to the pull of its strong sexual gravity. This is not to suggest that she labors under some perverse craving for subordination or abuse. Rather, the gunfighter's restrained but explosive nature seems replete with potent erotic promise. She is hardly alone in her response. We have noted the erotic element in Joe's reaction to Shane; clearly there is something of the same suppressed and deflected eros in Bob's. But the point to be made here is that while Shane exerts a magnetic attraction on men and women alike, he is himself apparently exempt from the sway of the desire that he triggers in others. This restores us to the paradox of Shane the inadvertent subverter of his own virtuous example. For although he takes it upon himself to preserve the warm, wholesome integrity of home, Shane's "natural" sexual allure is at the root of the worst of the trouble in Bob's homestead paradise.

Bob is hardly conscious of this ironic contradiction; indeed, his narrative may be said to dramatize the extremity of his wish to deny it. But his behavior betrays what consciousness rejects. It is the freedom from sexual contamination that Bob emphasizes in his final observations on Shane. The gunfighter has sacrificed himself in order that Bob may have the "chance to live out his boyhood and grow straight inside as a man should" (273). Shane knows "what goes on in a boy's mind and what can help him stay clean inside through the muddled, dirtied years of growing up" (262). The strong suggestion of disgust with adolescence and the onset of sexual "dirtiness" takes reinforcement from the example of the adults in Bob's world. He is witness to his mother's errant sexual maneuvering; most crucially, perhaps, he looks on when Marian asks Shane, "Are you doing this just for me?" (245). The vanity of the question, and the clearly implied invitation to greater intimacy, and therefore the advance toward more complete betrayal, cannot be entirely lost on the narrator. Bob also observes the erosion of his father's confidence and self-esteem in Shane's towering presence. He is the recorder of Joe's acquiescence in Marian's rationalizations, and of his personal initiative in the furtive game of deception. When Bob first asks, "Could you beat Shane? In a fight, I mean" (122), Joe equivocates. The boy doesn't ask again. But he hears Joe admit that Shane is the "better" man, and he is present when his father declares, "It helps a man to know that if anything happens to him, his family will be in better hands than his own" (238). Joe's beaten tone, his virtual invitation to death, and the clearly implied surrender to Shane, the superior man, are testimony to the heavy wages of adult sexual awareness. Bob must see, as his father certainly does, that Shane can have his way with Marian. The boy looks on while his mother is "watching Shane," and he observes "her throat curving in a lovely proud line, her eyes wide with a sweet warmth shining in them" (244). There is an ample measure of oedipal energy flowing through this passage, though it is safely sublimated in Shane and then fully checked in his rejection of Marian's implied offer. But Bob admires what he cannot have, while Shane may admire but he does not finally want. This difference distinguishes Shane from Bob, as it distinguishes him from all others. His imperial sexual authority, in combination with his immunity from sexual temptation, is the chief ingredient in his gathering influence with Bob, as it is in his progressive diminishment of Marian and Joe. The gunfighter's gathering contempt for farming—"You're a farmer," he belittles one of the neighbors, "that's all you ever will be" (210)—is evident. But "already," Bob admits, midway in Chapter 1, "I was imagining myself in hat and belt and boots like those" (67). By novel's end, Marian and Joe seem fallible and helpless and small, while the exemplary hero has become a god to their son.

This constellation of cognate tensions and downright contradictions may be said to aggregate in the management of point of view from the very beginning of *Shane*. In Bob's self-presentation, and in his aversion to the mysteries of adult behavior, we have the leading symptoms of the novel's profound rejection of sexuality, and its cognate subversion of the domestic ideal advanced on its surface. To the snags and tangles of domesticity, most especially as they are manifest in varieties of erotic maneuvering, Bob delivers a resounding, if not fully conscious, no. As I have tried to show, this recoil from the adult exigencies of his parents' lives, set in motion and fueled by Shane's example, is most persistently manifest in his repeated reminders that he does not fully comprehend his own story. Once recognized in the

CHAPTER 4

larger movements of the narrative, this habit of denial, and the pattern of opposition that it engenders, becomes discernible as well in the numerous lesser ambiguities and ironic contradictions that crop up everywhere in the novel. There is, for example, the clear drift toward a romantic inflection in Bob's memory of his mother as "the freshest, prettiest thing I had ever seen" (95). There is Marian's early, guarded ("murmured") expression of ambiguous concern about equally ambiguous motives with regard to Shane: "I hope Joe knows what he's doing" (98). And there is Joe's quite as richly ambiguous celebration of Shane's decision to stay and work at the homestead: "Marian, the sun's shining mighty bright at last. We've got ourselves a man" (118). Much later, when the battles have all been won, but Shane has gone away, Joe is strangely depressed. "Marian, I'm sick of the sight of this valley and all that's in it. If I tried to stay here now, my heart wouldn't be in it any more." The real excitement, the exhilarating struggle and the warm fellowship, comes to an abrupt halt with Shane's departure. Quotidian domestic life, with its assured future of small pleasures and its burden of mingled, often compromising memories, looks flat to Joe. What he really wanted, he senses, is gone. But what Marian really wanted has now been secured, and she will not consider leaving.

> "So you'd run out on Shane just when he's really here to stay?"
> "But, Marian. You don't understand. He's gone."
> "He's not gone. He's here, in this place, in this place he gave us. He's all around us and in us, and he always will be."
> She ran to the tall corner post, to the one Shane had set. She beat at it with her hands. "Here, Joe. Quick. Take hold. Pull it down." (270)

In the tall, wonderfully—comically—ambiguous post, Marian and Joe see and take hold of as much of Shane as is necessary to keep them both in the valley.

5

Characteristically, Marian is inclined to represent as a gift ("this place he gave us") what was, more properly, taken in spite of the benefactor's reluctance to give. This reminder of her self-interested inclination to ignore Shane's hesitation at the prospect of violence, in combination with her very telling instincts in the matter of symbolic memorials, may stir some suspicion that there was more than right-thinking respect for the all-American family in Shane's mind when he made his abrupt, very final departure. This is to suggest that an array of hitherto unlooked-for ironies may run through Shane's seemingly unequivocal last words to Bob. In declaring that "there's only one thing more I can do for them now," Shane means to spare the Starretts the stigma of the violent bloodletting. He will bear the burden of the trouble away with him, leaving the family ideally equipped for the righteous rearing of young Bob. But Shane's words may also betray an awareness that his presence in the valley has brought out weaknesses in Joe and Marian as individuals, and as a couple. Thus his departure will help them to stop hurting themselves. Finally, submerged in motives that surface only obliquely in his words, Shane may be leaving in order to protect his initiative and integrity. He has no love for farmers and farming, and he has had ample opportunity to see what is unlovable in the Starretts. He has bent more than once under the weight of Joe's need. He has been uneasy in Marian's attention to his exploits, and in her indifference to his reluctance as a fighter. He has had occasion to observe the inauthenticity of her gestures of intimacy, and the concealed self-interest of her appeals on Joe's behalf. Finally, he has listened to Joe admit that he is willing to die, and that he is quite content in the bargain to leave Marian to the "better" man. Hearing these words, Shane gets up "so swiftly that his chair . . . knocked against the wall" (238). Does he rise at this moment to Joe's defense? or does he in fact rise to protect himself from Marian—who, he may observe, raises no objection to her husband's words—and from the rest of the diminished legacy that Joe has written into his resigned scenario?

We can hardly doubt that Shane's loyalty to Joe figures prominently in his decision to fight. But the evidence just summarized gives weight to the inference that he is concerned as well to sidestep the burden of responsibility that Joe all but threatens to leave behind. There is added support for this line of interpretation in Shane's deft management of Marian's most overt advance toward sexual intimacy. As the final showdown draws near, she insists that it is time for them both to be completely frank. She has a "right to know" his feelings, she says; "And what I do depends on what you tell me now." Then she asks him if it is for her sake alone that he is going to face Fletcher

CHAPTER 4

and Wilson. "Shane hesitated for a long, long moment" (245). He must see, as we do, that Marian is inviting an affirmative answer. Why else ask the question? Does he go on to consider her probable responses to such an answer? We must suppose that he does. Why else hesitate for "a long, long moment"? There is little reason for him to suppose that Marian will now modestly decline what she has hitherto grasped for in spite of his manifest hesitation to give it. Still, she has made it clear that his response will somehow influence her own next step. Does she mean to suggest that she is prepared to answer his declaration of love with the proposal that they run away together, leaving Joe and Bob and the homestead behind? This is the only condition on which she would be likely to release him from his commitment to fight; thus it is the only plausible inference to be drawn from her indication that she will be guided by his answer. She will have her home, or she will have Shane. Unwilling to risk an open declaration of love (which could cost her everything), but unable to completely restrain desire, she contrives to make her shocking proposal without jeopardizing the farm. In effect, she forces Shane to choose for her. Little wonder that his answer is no.

This is what Shane ponders, I think, in his long pause. He sees what Marian is angling for, and he sees that she will take what she wants only if he shares the initiative and the moral responsibility for the choice. He may be shocked at what she seems to propose; he may be shocked that she imagines he might be tempted to go along. It may occur to him that he is only one of the two bases she has comfortably covered. In any case, her questions would seem to lend general confirmation to what he has suspected about Marian from the beginning. After another pause, and as if in response to her subtle maneuvering, he asks a question of his own, one heavy with apt, answering ambiguity. "No, Marian," he says, "Could I separate you in my mind and afterwards be a man?" (246)

Of course, we have no objective basis for certainty about what Shane thinks or intends during this exchange. I have proposed what strikes me as the most fully complete and plausible account of the appearances. In any case, it is the effect of Shane's response to obstruct Marian's invitation to intimacy and betrayal, and to confirm his own commitment to confront Fletcher and Wilson in Joe's place. Shane may be reluctant to risk more violence, but he is even more reluctant, his answer clearly suggests, to in any way multiply or tighten the ties that bind him to Marian. He would rather fight than do that. And, indeed, there is good evidence that deep down, all of his agonizing to the contrary notwithstanding, what Shane really wants is a fight. Something in him regrets violence, but something in him craves it even more. Shane is most naturally and completely himself, we have observed, when he is engaged in physical conflict. This is what he seems to have been made for. "Belt and holster and gun," Bob observes, "were not things he was wearing or carrying. They were part of him, part of the man, of the full sum of the integrate force that was Shane" (241). The hero may resist, but when the punching and shooting start, he is always there.

Nor, I think, is he self-deceived in this. He feels even more fully than we do the gusto that he brings to a fight; he laughs openly, and with evident, unembarrassed pleasure in the very midst of the fray. But again, some of the best evidence on this score, as on others we have reviewed, emerges as an ironic, subversive implication from beneath the surface of Bob's blandly repressed narrative. Consider the final verbal exchange between the ranchers and the homesteaders, a tense round of close calls with gunplay in which Wilson threatens Joe: "Think it over. You wouldn't like someone else to be enjoying this place of yours—and that woman there in the window" (232). Once the villains have drawn away, Joe and Shane take turns thanking each other for the risks they have just taken on each other's behalf. "He'd have drilled you, Joe," Shane insists,

> before you could have brought the gun up and pumped in a shell.
> "But you, you crazy fool!" Father was covering his feelings with a show of exasperation. "You'd have made him plug you just so I'd have a chance to get him." (234)

In the face of this barely restrained overflow of loving gratitude, Marian "jumped up.

> She pushed me aside. She flared at them from the doorway. "And both of you would have acted like fools just because he said that about me. I'll have you two know that if it's got to be done, I can take being insulted just as much as you can."
> Peering around her, I saw them gaping at her in astonishment. "But, Marian," father objected mildly, coming to her. "What better reason could a man have?"

CHAPTER 4

> "Yes," said Shane gently. "What better reason?" He was not looking just at mother. He was looking at the two of them. (234)

Marian is both upset and flattered that the men have put themselves in danger on her account. But she is also quite evidently jealous that Joe and Shane have totally controlled the action and that they are now totally absorbed in each other as the result. Though she does not say so directly, her abruptness and her words betray that she resents being left out.

Nor can she be very reassured by their response. The men's utter surprise at her reaction simply confirms what she deeply objects to in the relations of power. And while both men insist that she is eminently worthy of their exertions, their words also convey the suggestion that her worth as a person cannot be entirely separated from her value as an occasion for exhilarating rounds of muscle-flexing and intense brotherhood of the kind that they have just so evidently enjoyed. One must suppose that this suggestion is merely afloat in Joe's response. But the same words coming from Shane seem subtly to underscore what is merely nascent in her husband's reply. In the light of all that we know of the gunfighter's suspicion of Marian, and of his pleasure in violence, his repetition of "better reason" may seem a not so gently mocking euphemism for "excuse." This impression grows even stronger when Shane makes his emphatic adjustment in visual field, expanding his focus to include both members of the couple. This gesture bears with it an implicit rejection of Marian's assumption that he has acted solely on her behalf. Here as later in the novel, this deflationary thrust to Marian's vanity is found in combination with the familiar appeal to the family as the true object of the hero's self-sacrifice. But here as elsewhere this appeal seems rhetorical. For as this episode and many others make clear, and as Marian sees, the real excitement, the real motive and pull, is between the men; and even more fundamentally, it is in the fighting itself. "All the other stuff"—as Lawrence observed of Shane's type—the family, Bob, "the love . . . the foundering into lust," even the brotherhood with Joe, "is a sort of by-play." At the center of it all, straining for release, is "the integral soul" of the American hero, It is the soul of a man like Shane, who finally "turns his back on white society. A man who keeps his moral integrity hard and intact. An isolate, almost selfless, stoic, enduring man, who lives by death, by killing, but who is pure white.

This is the very intrinsic-most American. He is at the core of all the other flux and fluff. And when *this* man breaks from his static isolation, and makes a new move, then look out, something will be happening."[13]

6

These familiar words may serve to suggest that Shane gets precisely what he wants from his sojourn at the homestead. From the very outset he recognizes the potential for violence; he does not leave until all the fighting is over; but then he leaves immediately, and for good. This is the action that he craves. At the same time, it seems clear that his other activities at the homestead are very pleasurable adjuncts to the main business. He enjoys his brief comradeship with Joe; he is genuinely warm in his response to Marian; he is obviously fond of Bob. The return on this human investment is of course very great. All of the Starretts respond to him with emphatic, unmingled adoration. He knows this, but he does not allow his own feelings, or the love that others feel for him, to obscure the way to his primary objectives.

It is not in Shane's nature to tolerate more than a minimum of intimacy. Deep down, as I have tried to show, he is suspicious of people, shy of company, remote from family, inclined to celibacy. This side of him speaks to the Calvinism in our culture, to a fundamental distrust of human beings, especially in groups. It may help to account for his violent predilections, and for the fact that in helping people he always diminishes them at the same time. Shane's power—the combination in him of physical authority and charisma—is so complete and commanding that it dwarfs the resources of others, and in fact draws out their weaknesses. Thus his friendship with Joe is hardly one of equals; indeed, it prompts Joe to varieties of selfishness and deceit that would ordinarily be beneath him. Marian is also less than her best self in Shane's presence. She so desires what he has that she is reduced to deceit and seduction, and tempted to the verge of betrayal. This diminishment of Joe and Marian must be obvious to Shane. But he gives no sign of surprise or disillusionment at what he sees. He knows what people are, and he moves among them in a manner that draws attention to his own moral purity, reinforces his inclination to shy away, gives cause to his impulse to leave, and—most vitally—justifies his violence as necessary, and even dignifies it as self-sacrifice. Closely attuned as it is to his "natural" recoil from intimacy, Shane's power serves to align all of the "by-play" with his pleasure, and thus to underpin the larger economy of his heroism. Power, it is fair to say, is the key to it all. Because he has it, Shane gets everything—love, complete independence, clean hands, adventure, violence—that he wants; because they lack it, and because it gets away from them, the Starretts must settle for their diminished homestead and their diminished selves.

Shane's feelings in all of this are rarely more than hinted at. The gunfighter is the least developed of the major characters in the novel. In fact, it is precisely this lack of development, this paucity of psychological detail, that accounts for his supremely elevated stature. As Swift and Nietzsche well knew, the subjection of individuals to close, sustained scrutiny leads invariably to the erosion of ordinary assumptions about human dignity. Mankind cannot bear too much inspecting. This has certainly been confirmed in our careful analysis of the members of the All-American family in *Shane*. It is not without reason that the hero is comparatively flat. We may wonder if he is naturally this way, or whether his two-dimensionality is in fact the guarded expression of a higher shrewdness, a manifestation of a deeply self-interested refusal to give anything away. In any case, it is power and purity that finally matter. And they matter first, and perhaps most, to Bob. After all, Shane is Bob's creation; and his leading qualities, even to his conspicuous lack of depth, must be understood primarily in their relation to his maker. This is to return, of course, to the recognition that Shane's character is an oblique index to Bob's disillusionment with mother and father and home and love and human beings generally. Clearly enough, the onset of this permanent disenchantment came at that interval in his life when childhood gave way to adolescence, and when he first glimpsed what he subsequently came to regard as "the muddled, dirtied" realities of adult life. It is perfectly ironic, but also perfectly compatible with the dynamics of heroic power, that Shane's example should have intensified the boy's adolescent disillusionment and at the same time eroded completely his confidence in its ostensible antidote—as specifically endorsed by the gunfighter—home. Thus in casting himself as Bob's benefactor, the hero diminishes him, too, with the result that the Shane of fantasy and memory is not so much the preserver of home as he is the agent and potent alternative to domestic, and more broadly social, disenchantment. In his flatness, his impenetrable exteriority, Shane is proof against both self-subversion and disillusionment. Viewed in this light, his narrative is a fantasy of retreat from contaminating, disenchanting human intimacy into isolated, independent, stoical, murderous purity. There was a time, Bob reflects, when he wanted to be like his father. But now "I was not so sure. I wanted more and more to be like Shane, like the man I imagined he was in the past fenced off so securely. I had to imagine most of it. He would never speak of it, not in any way at all. Even his name remained mysterious. Just Shane. Nothing else" (134).

7

Bob is hardly alone in his failure to penetrate fully the significance of the mysterious cowboy who has passed through his life. The published criticism of the novel has been dominated by attention to broad historical and mythic considerations—the frontier, America's coming of age, the claims of civilization in the new land—and correspondingly inattentive to the subversive drift of much textual detail. Gerald Haslam, drawing on "Frederick Jackson Turner via Roy Allen Billington," argues that *Shane* illustrates the frontier pattern of "herdsmen roaming ahead of the line of settlement, pioneering unwittingly for the very farmers who would drive them from their lands."[4] Fred Erisman, using Clinton Rossiter's profile of nationhood as his yardstick, takes the view that *Shane* dramatizes the achievement of "territorial integrity, popular cohesion, independence, and self-identity."[5] And Michael Cleary, turning from Rossiter back to Turner, finds that "Shane's utilization of his savage skills . . . simultaneously secures the values of civilization and alienates him from it."[6] These are valuable perspectives on the novel. They point to the kinds of broadly American themes that Schaefer must have had in mind as he approached his story. At the same time, however, the nearly schematic quality in such historical readings works to flatten nuance and ambiguity, to neutralize irony, and to reduce the text to a kind of two-dimensional allegory of American progress across the continent.

This critical predilection is not, I think, merely the reflection of academic fashion. Rather, it is part and parcel with Bob's failure to fully grasp the significance of his own narrative. The critical response recapitulates Bob's denial of discord and disenchantment because it shares his fundamental cultural disinclination to come to a reckoning with those elements in the story. This is to suggest that Bob speaks for Americans not only or even primarily in the kind of story he tells but also in the way that he organizes and highlights and obscures what he was to say. Bob speaks for us because his complex construction of reality, with its revelations and concealments, its simultaneous telling and un-telling, its very specific dynamic of repression, fully anticipates our own deeply cultural habits of mind. *Shane* is ours not because the gunfighter is one of us, but because Bob is, and because his range of assumptions about family and self and sexuality and society, and the tensions that work to color and strain those assumptions, are in fundamental consonance with those of his audience and serve to cast light on some of the key areas of stress and contradiction in American culture. Broad historical and mythic themes cannot in themselves account for the potent appeal of Bob's narrative, for the ways in which we are drawn to and powerfully moved by this familiar, even weary and utterly implausible story. But we fail to locate the novel's deeper, rather vague center of attraction because we do not really want to. Indeed, it is the evasion of that center, the successful skirting of painful revelations, the close calls with conscious disenchantment, that makes us feel in tune and in touch, and that keep us coming back. Bob's story is a compulsive recounting of a childhood episode much of whose impact was no sooner felt than deflected, no sooner glimpsed than banished from sight and mind. But his story also registers the return of his repressed disenchantment with father and mother and home. He tells it all again because he must, just as we witness it again and again, in this story and in countless others just like it, because we must. We are compelled to this repetition because, as the vast popular reception of *Shane* clearly indicates, we accept into consciousness only those elements of the narrative that conform to a culturally preferred conception of home and heroism. The rest, the messiness and maneuvering, the selfishness and sexual by-play, we are strongly inclined, following Bob, to repress. Thus the impulse to deny may be said to tell the tale, though the denial in turn assures that we will pass this way again.

8

This view of *Shane* is cognate in a number of ways with the rather more indirect commentary set forth by E. L. Doctorow in *Welcome to Hard Times*. I like to think that Doctorow was reading *Shane* during the hours that he took off from the composition of his own western novel; in fact, he might have been reading, or thinking about, or watching on television, any one of an endless procession of virtual replicas of the formula that *Shane* embodies. Doctorow's analysis is broadly cultural because the essentials of his story are very familiar. He makes his case by working conspicuously within the formula but drawing its drift and implications out to unfamiliar extremes. The violence-prone hero in *Welcome to Hard Times* is a tornado of ceaseless, motiveless, unrepentant destruction, and the female protagonist, Molly, is an abused, degraded, ruthlessly grasping, and manipulative prostitute. The two of them are locked in a kind of ferocious marriage of blistering, galvanizing antipathy. It is an extreme variation on the submerged female/male thematics of the conventional heroic narrative. When the denying is finally over and the truth is finally revealed, Doctorow seems to suggest, this is the way it is between the men and the women in one of our favorite stories.

The narrator of *Welcome to Hard Times*, a man named Blue, is by far the most fully developed of the novel's characters. Doctorow's emphasis on the teller is his way of underscoring the essential constructedness of the very familiar, if very extreme, world that he sets before us. Blue is clearly akin to Bob Starrett. He is a narrator whose tale registers dark insights that never seem to surface fully in his consciousness. He is bland and matter of fact in describing a sordid, violent, doomed society. To the very end Blue keeps ledgers, written accounts of events as they unfold. The writing seems to provide a measure of control, distance, and hope. It reinforces Blue's sense of himself as an embattled innocent. But all of this, Doctorow makes clear, is false. The only things under control in the town of Hard Times are the narrator's carefully cultivated illusions. In fact, Blue is up to his writing hand in the hopeless world that he surveys. His innocence is a sham, a cover for spineless evasions and an imperfectly repressed fascination with the bloodletting. Thus his story, like Bob's, is a continuous and circular process of seeing and concealing, recording and denying, a recoil from experience into a consoling but utterly fabricated web of words.

Blue's self-deception is nowhere more extreme than in his attempt to join with Molly and a damaged orphan boy as the first new family in the town that the predatory outlaw has just destroyed. The parallels with the submerged domestic dynamics in *Shane* add up to a darkly ironic commentary on Schaefer's representation of the all-American family. This strange new Adam and Eve in their barren garden of ashes have their nucleus not in Blue but in the Bad Man, who embodies the massive and finally uncontrolled violence and sexual energy that they have buried in themselves. The reminders of *Shane* are perhaps most irresistible in the boy, whose filial regard for the brutal rapist, and manifest calling as the next Bad Man, are the direct expression of an extreme oedipal urge. The family stays together only because its individual members wait together for the return, in the Bad Man, of repressed parts of themselves. When he arrives, Blue, like Joe, finally gets an exhilarating fight; with Marian, Molly has her chance to vie for parity with men; with Bob, the orphan boy finds a role model in the gunfighter. Confronted once again with the collapse of his illusions, Blue, like Bob in *Shane*, retreats to his ledgers, and to yet another verbal reconstruction of a diminished reality.

"Fiction," Doctorow has observed, "is a not entirely rational means of discourse. It gives to the reader something more than information. Complex understandings, indirect, intuitive, and nonverbal, arise from the words of the story, and by a ritual transaction between reader and writer, instructive emotion is generated in the reader from the illusion of suffering an experience not his own. A novel is a printed circuit through which flows the force of a reader's own life."[7] This view of the essential collaboration of writer and reader in the fabrication of meaning clearly anticipates my own analysis of the dynamics of reader recapitulation in the popular response to books like *Shane*. As applied to *Welcome to Hard Times*, Doctorow's commentary finds its focus in Blue, whose ledgers are specimens of "fiction" and emphatically not an "entirely rational means of discourse." Blue is first and foremost a writer, and writers know, Doctorow insists, "that the world in which we live is still to be formed and that reality is amenable to any construction that is placed upon it. It is a world made for liars and we are born liars."[8] Quite as obviously, Blue exemplifies the grave perils of fictional world-building. Here as elsewhere Doctorow seems strongly inclined to a psychosexual approach to history; for *Welcome to Hard Times* offers itself as a warning against the attempt, in civilization, to achieve stability by repressing powerful and potentially destructive energies and impulses. The construction of reality is here characterized as an activity dominated by omission, concealment, evasion, and self-deception. But, Doctorow makes clear, the disposition to deny is broadly based. In its implied commentary on the authority of the Western formula story, *Welcome to Hard Times* implicates the reader in the culturally sanctioned, virtually obligatory refabrication of a fragile construction of reality. It is fragile because so much of the constructing involves conspicuous denial; it is obligatory because the repressed discordancies and contradictions are forever pressing up against the surface of consciousness. "And now," Blue concludes, "I've put down what happened, everything that happened from one end to the other. And it scares me more than death scares me that it may show the truth."[9]

5

THEORETICAL POSTSCRIPT

1

Drawing on these works by Grey, Cooper, Wister, London, and Schaefer, and on others by Mark Twain, I want now to take a broader view of the patterns of denial that surface in popular American fiction. All of these novels, I have argued, tell two stories, not just one; and the "parts" so divided work in a paradoxical and self-subversive way to reveal what they conceal, to affirm what they deny, to deny what they affirm. Our texts strongly suggest that this is a complicated process—as complicated as Blue's deathly fear that his chronicle may somehow reveal the truth. His compulsion to inscribe obeys a mysterious, divided impulse to reveal some vaguely glimpsed truth, and, at the same time, a countering impulse to conceal it. Schaefer, Grey, Cooper, Twain, and the others, I have found, are doing something of the same thing. Yet *Welcome to Hard Times* and Doctorow's observations on fiction bear the clear suggestion that the reader, like the teller of the tale—the born liar—will settle for a partial, incomplete construction of the truth before him on the page. The readers of *Shane* and our other novels, I want to argue, have generally done the same thing. I will go further and suggest, as I think Doctorow does, that there is a clear relationship between the conscious, surface narrative and the submerged, subversive material it conceals. The plausible, perfectly predictable surface of the tale answers the need to obscure yet once more a contrary, subversive perspective whose persistent resurgence on the margins of consciousness—and of the narrative—ensures that the tale will require repeating, and will thereby achieve popularity. What then are we to make of the fact that all of these novels

CHAPTER 5

bear witness to a strong, evidently unconscious impulse, shared by author/narrators and readers alike, to be deceived?

In raising this question—or, more precisely, the array of questions that this question implies—I am resuming and substantially elaborating on the discussion in my book, *In Bad Faith: The Dynamics of Deception in Mark Twain's America*. In that study, and in others that have followed from it,[1] I have detected a pattern of recapitulating evasions that I define as *bad faith*, the deception of self and other in the denial of violations of public ideals of truth and justice. Such departures, as they appear in Mark Twain's work, are most frequently group phenomena, collaborative denials, and bear with them the clear implication that people will sometimes permit or acquiesce in what they cannot approve, so long as their complicity is submerged in a larger, tacit consensus. Let me stress that bad faith is not always bad. In its benign and even beneficial phase, it enables a society to transcend the strict letter of its codes and the unanticipated limitations of its actors and circumstances. But it may also work to conceal problems of grave consequence. Mark Twain was sharply aware of the social unity and fellow-feeling to be derived from the deception of self and other, but he was equally attentive to the pathologies of bad faith. In either form, however, it is a telling feature of acts of bad faith that they incorporate silent prohibitions against the acknowledgment that they have occurred—denial is itself denied.

My definition of bad faith takes rise from the close analysis of village social dynamics as they are represented in *Tom Sawyer*. I find that Mark Twain's characters are engaged in an elaborate form of social play whose dominant feature is the reciprocal deception of self and other in the denial of departures from leading public values. The term *bad faith* is also applied to the cognate pattern of denial that emerges in Mark Twain's handling of his materials, and that may be observed as well in the audience reception of his books. Thus the cultural dynamics observable in the action of the novel are repeated in the telling and in the response to the tale.

The recapitulating levels of bad faith witnessed in the complex, generally comical and benign world of *Tom Sawyer* reappear, now in a more pathological form, in *Huckleberry Finn*. Once again, bad faith is everywhere to be observed—in the behavior of people in towns along the river, but also in the young hero himself, in his author's management of the story, and in the novel's enduring popular reception. At the root of this pervasive malady is race-slavery, an institution whose maintenance in a Christian democracy requires extraordinary bad faith denial and whose existence over time fosters a wide range of kindred deceptions. The culminating episode in this darkly emergent cultural portrait is Tom's famous "evasion," the ostensibly humorous freeing of an already free man. Here as elsewhere in his writing, Mark Twain's approach to the tormented heart of his fictional enterprise intersects with a countering impulse toward distraction. The urge to tell the unbearable truth about Huck and Jim and their world arrives at a culturally revealing impasse with the urge to laugh it all off. This retreat from painful implication is also manifest in the history of the novel's halting composition, and in the enormous appetite for violent distraction among its leading actors. The same may be said of the enduring and widespread reader approval of *Huckleberry Finn*, a response arising out of pleasure that is itself the uncertain issue of Tom's evasion. At all these levels, then, *Huckleberry Finn* records or prompts a movement toward resolution, never completed, with nightmare. The dark implications of race-slavery press upward against the surface of the narrative, or of consciousness, only to be pressed down, and to rise and fall again and again in a repeating cycle of bad faith denial.

In what must be obvious ways, the results of my study of Mark Twain anticipate and even inform what I find in the works analyzed here. These are also texts that reflect an impulse, in their author/narrators and in their audience, to submerge nagging discord and contradiction. But that impulse in turn points to a countering drive to address painful questions of value. Cooper is at some level deeply troubled by the "Indian problem"; Grey, London, and Schaefer are in rather different ways concerned with sexual inequality. Thus the evasive tendency is always found in combination with its opposite, and the negotiation of the tension between such opposed tendencies may be said to drive the narrative. I want to stress that no two texts manage the tension in exactly the same way. *Tom Sawyer* is apparently untroubled by serious ambiguity, whereas the seemingly confident management of contradiction in *Shane* is subtly belied by the halting tone of the narrator himself. *Huckleberry Finn* and *The Sea-Wolf*, on the other hand, are conspicuously divided throughout, and conclude with gestures of decided ambiguity. But although the nature and dynamics of the dominant tensions vary from text to text, it is nonetheless safe to generalize that the novels are never open-and-shut affairs in which discord and contradiction are revealed only to be resubmerged at the close of the narrative. The contrary impulses to see and not see, to address painful issues and to turn away from them, are always delicately, dialectically poised in these texts, and never fully "managed" or resolved. Indeed, it is the very essence of the appeal of these novels that they are rehearsals of unfinished cultural business. They are quite direct in their approach to issues such as racism and sexual inequality; they help us to live with these problems, and not simply by ignoring them or by subtly maneuvering them out of sight and mind.

With *Tom Sawyer* and *Huckleberry Finn*, then, the novels assembled here enjoy large audiences precisely because of their *simultaneous* approach to and retreat from leading cultural contradictions. To the extent that these writers share Mark Twain's preoccupation with racism and slavery, their works feature kindred varieties of moral evasion. I want to emphasize (what must already be obvious), however, that in moving beyond Mark Twain I have found that popular renderings of the relations between the sexes entail evasive strategies of representation quite similar to those accorded racial issues in novels such as *Huckleberry Finn*. This comes as no surprise. Bad faith is almost certainly at work wherever the embarrassed relations between social practices and leading cultural ideals are, by whatever means, and for whatever apparent reasons, somehow rendered obscure.

In further elaborating on the literary and cultural significance of these popular novels, I will review and, wherever possible, borrow from a representative body of theoretical writing on culture, popular culture, ideology, cultural poetics, audience response, the social construction of reality, and other related topics. My objective in this is to pull together some of the major elements of a theory of popular literature as that theory emerges from and finds endorsement in the works that I have studied closely. Here as elsewhere my point of departure and emphatic center of attention is the text itself. From the outset it must be clear that the evidence advanced here will not support the view that popular texts win audience approval by the facile resolution of cultural or ideological contradictions; nor does it reinforce theories that cast the reader as a passive tool of ideological manipulation. These and other questions will turn up again in what follows. But let me add by the way of introduction a few of the assumptions, grounded in my experience of popular texts and confirmed by reading in secondary materials, that inform my critical position.[2]

Popular literature, like Shakespearean theater, is "not merely the passive reflector of social forces that lay entirely outside of it; rather," as Stephen Greenblatt argues, the theater, "like all forms of art, indeed like all utterances," is "itself a *social event*. Artistic expression is never perfectly self-contained and abstract, nor can it be derived satisfactorily from the subjective consciousness of an isolated creator. Collective actions, ritual gestures, paradigms of relationship, and shared images of authority penetrate the work of art and shape it from within, while conversely the socially overdetermined work of art, along with a multitude of other institutions and utterances, contributes to the formation, realignment, and transmission of social practices."[3] Art is in a dialectical relation to society. The artist and the audience are constituted by the social context that they in turn help to form and modify. Art, the artist, and the audience have a similar relationship to history, which is never accessible in its pure or real state, but is always present to consciousness in a mediated form. Such mediation is the work of culture and ideology, terms freighted with the assumption that the world is meaningful, and with the array of meanings—always partial, distorted, contradictory, incomplete—duly conceived. Popular art is popular precisely because of its simultaneous challenge to and confirmation of the "natural" and the taken-for-granted. In adopting this latter position, I betray my broader assumption (here following Fredric Jameson) that "the literary work or cultural object, as though for the first time, brings into being that very situation to which it is also, at one and the same time, a reaction."[4]

2

Jameson's magisterial theoretical position has at its center a conception of the text as divided between a distorted surface and a concealed but critically retrievable lower layer. It follows that the "process of criticism is not so much an interpretation of content as it is a revealing of it, a laying bare, a restoration of the original message, the original experience, beneath the distortions of the various kinds of censorship that have been at work upon it; and this revelation takes the form of an explanation of why the content was so distorted and is thus inseparable from a description of the mechanisms of this censorship itself."[5]

In due course I will attempt a more detailed alignment of my findings with Jameson's views on "mass culture." For now I want to seize upon his emphasis on the dividedness of the cultural object. Though there is a very marked disagreement among observers about the sources of this division, and about the characteristics of the elements so divided, there is something approaching consensus that the cultural object, variously defined, is binary and oppositional in structure. This is to say that cultural texts of many kinds may be expected, when carefully analyzed, to fall into two parts or planes related spatially as surface to depth and logically as contradictory opposites.[6] Obviously the novels that I have in mind here fit quite tidily into this pattern. *The Last of the Mohicans* bears on its face an array of boundaries—racial, cultural, linguistic, sexual—that it works, at another level, to undermine. *Riders of the Purple Sage, The Virginian,* and *The Sea-Wolf* are divided in their representation of the hero and offer what may be viewed as an ironic subtextual characterization of the heroine. At one level *Shane* celebrates the family ideal, at another it reveals its grave contradictions. *Huckleberry Finn* overlays a story of heroic liberation on a much darker tale of false hopes and failed impulses toward change. *Pudd'nhead Wilson* is superficially a chronicle of mystery resolved and order restored; more deeply, it ends where it begins, in dark, explosive secrecy. And *A Connecticut Yankee,* which takes life from a surge of confidence in American progress, is freighted with profound, but never fully acknowledged or articulated, doubts on the same score. In every text the divided, contradictory, self-subversive pattern reappears.

Our texts are also alike in other ways. They are all popular. They had large audiences at the time of their publication, and they have earned a permanent place on the shelf of books that Americans come back to. Moreover, and as I have already suggested, there is little evidence of sustained authorial or audience penetration into the divided, subversive texture of these narratives. This is not to conclude that writers and readers are totally unresponsive to the contradictions in some of their favorite books. Nor is it to suggest that such discordancies should be dismissed as excrescences. Quite the contrary, it is to acknowledge the presence of these divisive elements and to suggest that they are integral to the popularity of the texts in which they appear. Authors and readers return to these stories because they form the occasion for an active, virtually obligatory reencounter with primary cultural concerns (identity, freedom, the family, sexual politics, and so on) in which the affirmation of the familiar and taken-for-granted is accompanied by the denial of all that conflicts with that confident construction of reality. The denial of denial, it follows, is also an essential in this preeminently cultural behavior, for without it the fact of the text's constructedness would rudely undermine our pleasurable reconfirmation of "the natural." Indeed, it is our need to deny that explains the otherwise baffling demand for constant repetition of the familiar; and it is denial thus broadly defined, as integral to and in a sense constitutive of culture, that I refer to in the term *bad faith*.[7] But this is to get ahead of myself.

It must be obvious that the texts assembled here provide no support for the notion, common among students in the field, that popular literature involves "the construction of an ideal world without the disorder, the ambiguity, the uncertainty, and the limitations of the world of our experience."[8] The impulse to construct such a world is manifest in the novels I have studied, but a countering impulse, productive of ambiguity and uncertainty and a sense of limitation, is evident as well. Thus it cannot be said of these popular texts, as it is often said of popular texts generally—that they "resolve tensions and ambiguities resulting from the conflicting interests of different groups within the culture or from ambiguous attitudes toward particular values."[9] To be sure, such tensions and ambiguities and conflicts are addressed; indeed, their appearance, I have suggested, may be an indispensable ingredient in the formula for popularity. But they are hardly resolved. Rather, it is the failure of such resolution, and the denied presence of denial in its place, that characterizes these books, and that seems to figure in their deep cultural authority.

My study of novels like *Huckelberry Finn* and *Shane* thus predisposes me to favor commentary that acknowledges, and even highlights, the unresolved tensions and conflicts in popular texts. In fact, many critics and theorists do just this.[10] Clifford Geertz is well known for his insistence that "cultural integration is no longer taken to be a *sui generis* phenomenon locked away from the common life of man in a logical world of its own." Such encouragement to look for culture in the apparently random and everyday is, of course, well taken.

CHAPTER 5

So is the assurance that "the elements of a culture's own negation are, with greater or lesser force, included within it."[11] Most helpful of all perhaps is Geertz's sense that the appeal of popular expressive forms is rooted in their disarrangement of the taken-for-granted, not in its confirmation. Thus the "function" of popular forms—such as cockfights—"is interpretive"; they are stories, significantly contradictory and self-subversive, that people "tell themselves about themselves."[12] Culture, in this view, is available to us in the everyday, and it offers itself as a kind of dialogue in which contrary perspectives contend. Culture is expressed, and effectively—almost compulsively—reproduced, in the tense play of unresolved contradictions.

The "text is construed in related, albeit psychoanalytical, terms by Norman N. Holland, who finds that "all stories—and all literature—have this basic way of meaning: they transform the unconscious fantasy discoverable through psychoanalysis into the conscious meanings discovered by conventional interpretation." The production of meaning is "a dynamic process" in which "rather unsavory wishful or fearful fantasies" are reworked "into social, moral, or intellectual themes which are consciously satisfying to the ego and unconsciously satisfying to the deep wishes being acted out by the literary work." Such psychological maneuverings between opposite "places" and perspectives take place "not just in the literary work" (and, by implication, in its maker), "but also in us who have introjected them: transformation 'out there' is felt as transformation 'in here.'" Much of this applies directly to the popular texts before us. Literary meaning in them, as in literature more generally for Holland, is the product of an emphatically active maneuvering, by author, text, and audience, of elements in tension or opposition, whose negative pole or face is pressed "down" while the positive is advanced to the view. I would emphasize that this process does not culminate in resolution; to the contrary, it is the persistence of tension, temporarily veiled perhaps in the illusion of closure, that brings us back to our favorite books. This possible difference in emphasis notwithstanding, Holland's account of having "the fantasy and feeling it managed" clearly anticipates the experience that I have in mind.[13]

These points of contact with Holland serve to highlight the decidedly Freudian—which is to say, non-Sartrean—cast of my notion of bad faith. For it is to the Freudian scheme, with its attention to repression, latency, sublimation, condensation, reaction formation, and other mechanisms of distortion and concealment, that we most often turn to describe and account for the fact that we can know and seemingly fail to know the same things, tell and un-tell the same stories. "The essence of repression," Freud assures us, "lies simply in the function of rejecting and keeping something out of consciousness."[14] It is equally clear, however, that repressed fantasies are forever pressing upward against the surface of consciousness, aspiring to elude the censor that would restrain them. There is a rather striking parallel between these novels that manage (without quite knowing or revealing it) to have things both ways, and the Freudian dream, with its "(disguised) fulfillment of a (suppressed or repressed) wish."[15] Our dreams are always interested; they enable the ego to satisfy desires that it cannot bring itself to own. This evasive legerdemain succeeds because the distortions introduced by the dream-work are themselves concealed under plausible, distracting fictions. Strategic failures of memory have a part to play; so do familiar, apparently harmless dream elements that function as "cover" for intruders from the unconscious.[16] Like the texts assembled here, then, the dream is an oblique and measured mental encounter with resurgent, potentially distressing materials.

Having said this much, it is essential to add that the Freudian censor is primarily concerned to manage repressed childhood wishes, while the mechanisms of bad faith, as I have observed them in books like *The Last of the Mohicans* and *The Virginian,* are directed toward painful revelations in matters such as race and gender. Thus where Holland, following Freud quite directly, casts his analysis of literary meaning in a psychological framework, I am inclined to be much more social and historical, or cultural, in my point of departure. I hasten to add, however, that psychoanalytical elements have a place in my analysis, though only as adjuncts to the dominant social perspectives. Thus in *Shane,* as I view it, the general impulse to submerge discordant perspectives on the family has its correlative in Bob's repression of his oedipal designs on Marian. It is cognate with this difference in emphasis that Holland regards the literary transformation of unconscious fantasies as a form of psychological adaptation, while I tend to view the conscious surface of the text as an evasion of social issues. Again, without wishing to minimize real differences, I would reiterate that bad faith in its benign manifestations may be viewed as a mechanism of adaptation to unbending codes and customs. Such bad faith, I have argued (most especially in my analysis of *Tom Sawyer*), is a social good. In the case of *Shane*, the good and bad of the thing is nicely mingled; for although Bob's submergence of his oedipal fantasy may be viewed as a positive adaptation, its place in the more general evasion of major social problems may not. In any case, here—and even more so elsewhere—our texts offer the psychological as a correlative to the social, and not the other way around.

3

The application of Holland's psychoanalytic model to the social dimension in popular literature has been most notably evident in the work of Fredric Jameson. In his influential essay, "Reification and Utopia in Mass Culture," Jameson undertakes "to rewrite the concept of a management of desire in social terms." This "allows us," he goes on, "to grasp mass culture not as empty distraction or 'mere' false consciousness, but rather as a transformational work on social and political anxieties and fantasies which must then have some effective presence in the mass cultural text in order subsequently to be 'managed' or repressed." More specifically, Jameson argues that a trace of "genuine social and historical content" must be "given some initial expression" in works of mass culture before "ideological manipulation" can occur. This "bribe to the public about to be . . . manipulated" is "Utopian" in its evocation of "the deepest and most fundamental hopes of the collectivity." Public acquiescence in the diminished status quo is thus purchased at the price of a glimpse of that something better that it displaces.[17]

The relevance of Jameson's theoretical position to the texts studied here must be obvious. His emphasis on the oppositional structure of the text, his insistence that contradiction is rooted in competing social perspectives, and his acknowledgment of active audience involvement in the management of discord anticipate my own findings. Moreover, I take support in principle from his general view (developed elsewhere, but entirely in keeping with the argument of "Reification and Utopia") that "the production of aesthetic or narrative forms is to be seen as an ideological act in its own right, with the function of inventing imaginary or formal 'solutions' to unresolvable social contradictions."[18] Form manages or contains audience dissatisfaction by drawing attention away from the source of discord. A similar pattern surfaces in the novels studied here. In *Shane*, for example, the first-person narration of young Bob serves to submerge contradiction. The same may be said of the narrators in *Huckleberry Finn*, *The Virginian*, and *The Sea-Wolf*. In *Riders of the Purple Sage*, *The Last of the Mohicans*, and *Pudd'nhead Wilson*, generic exigencies (of the romance and the mystery novel) work to similar effect. But while form serves to manage contradiction in these texts, it does not do it in precisely the way that Jameson suggests it should. He finds that the submerged interior of the artifact is the positive pole of the oppositional structure; the "inside" contains the utopian conception of life that the "outside" manages. In my texts, however, the "preferred" view of the world tends toward the surface, while a competing, subversive perspective is pressed downward, though not completely out of sight. For Jameson, the fleeting glimpse of the submerged utopia is the lure that draws the audience in, and that forms the occasion for the deception. In novels like *Huckleberry Finn* and *Shane* and the others, however, I have found that the superficial resolution of tension is keyed to the imperfect suppression of persistent, much darker, and more faithful intimations of the real.

These differences in the disposition of the "parts" of the popular artifact point to other key points of disagreement. It must be clear, for example, that Jameson's audience is much more passive than mine. He conceives of readers or viewers as active only to the extent that they penetrate briefly to a glimpse of utopia; thereafter they are the passive subjects of "ideological manipulation." The mass cultural text is popular because it arouses and then promptly and thoroughly contains intolerable desire. My audience, on the contrary, joins the author/narrator and the text itself in the active bad faith denial of a resurgent, discordant challenge to the surface of the narrative. Audience acquiescence is thus a cultural phenomenon, a not involuntary entry into the broad, sweeping consensual flow, rather than supine surrender to a manipulative other. And the novels studied here, I argue, are popular because they move us toward a bearable angle of vision on matters that we can neither face for long nor fully forget.

The members of Jameson's audience are quite readily manipulated and deceived into submission to an ideology that does violence to their buried ideals. They are easily bribed. My audience, on the other hand, is self-manipulated and self-deceived. They participate, however unconsciously, in a compromise with their values, an evasion of the acknowledgment that they are not in all important ways faithful to their ideals. I am therefore not at all surprised to find that popular novels are characteristically tense with contradictions that surface, under critical analysis, in high relief. To the contrary, such often tortured inner division is the key to the cultural currency of the text, for it answers similar divisions in the teller of the tale, and in its audience. For Jameson the discovery of a socially redeeming dimension in texts otherwise dismissed as "degraded" is something of a scandal. "We cannot fully do justice to the ideological function of works like these," he writes, "unless we are willing to *concede* the presence within them of a more positive function as well" (italics added).[19] I emphasize "concede" because it is in just such a mood of evident reluctance that Jameson bends to his own critical imperatives. Such faint traces of the redeeming truth as appear in the "degraded" productions of mass culture are there, one senses, primarily by virtue of theoretical necessity. Allowing as we must for the difference between Jameson's "mass" culture and my own "popular" variety, it is still the case that he is strongly inclined to condemn all "ideological manipulation" as bad because it conceals what is authentic and good from its hapless audience.[20]

Whether its object is mass or popular culture, this is an extreme position driven, as I have suggested, by the exigencies of theory and, much more broadly, by a thoroughgoing hostility to the ways and means of capitalism. Mass culture is at once a leading agent and symptom of what Jameson regards as the alienation and dehumanization of modern existence, a disease brought on by "the corrosive and tradition-annihilating effects of the spread of a money and market economy."[21] It is the essential paradox of mass culture that in order to advance the interests of a corrupt ideology, it must also—and quite in spite of itself—offer us reminders, however scant and fleeting, of life "as we feel in our bones it ought . . . to be lived."[22] There is undoubtedly an ample measure of truth in this position; certainly there is evidence in the texts that Jameson analyzes, and in those scrutinized here, to support his general view. But if popular novels like *Shane* and *The Virginian*—not to mention *Tom Sawyer*, *The Sea-Wolf*, and the others—have any place in the analysis of mass culture, then Jameson's line of analysis, although penetrating and extremely valuable as a model, is also manifestly incomplete. For the evidence of these texts strongly suggests that "ideological distortion" is a broadly based cultural phenomenon embracing a multitude of concerns, involving active audience collaboration, and while typically evasive in strategy, not always pathological or bad in its bad faith. My texts tend to enforce a much more spacious and modulated conception of popular or mass culture than Jameson's. Based on my study of books like *Shane*, I am inclined to view the varieties of distortion in popular texts as representative of the operations of culture generally; versions of such evasion are to be found, I assume, in all species of cultural representation. At times, to be sure, the resistance to the truth of social and historical reality is a symptom of the pathology so denied and may be said to contribute to the persistence of the disease. This is the case, I have argued, in *Huckleberry Finn*. But I have also found that the bad faith in books, like the bad faith in the "real" world, varies quite considerably in its capacity for good and ill. Indeed, I want to go on to argue that bad faith is a leading constituent of culture and ideology and thus inescapably an ingredient in our experience of the world. But again, I am getting ahead of myself.

4

Jameson is not alone, of course, in developing the argument that capitalism is to be held responsible for the unique and extreme modern departure from the social order as it ought to be and as it ought, therefore, to appear. Louis Althusser's view of ideology as "the imaginary relationship of individuals to the real conditions of existence" is obviously cognate with Jameson's, and as obviously relevant in a general sort of way to the texts studied here. But Althusser's insistence that ideologies "always express *class positions*" conflicts with our reading of novels that highlight racial and sexual boundaries and that draw upon tensions emergent from within, and not simply between, social groups.[23] His emphasis on the passivity of the bearer of ideology ("the subject acts insofar as he is acted by the . . . system") and on the notion "that ideology *has no outside* (for itself)," is similarly at odds with the evidence, assembled here, of active (if not fully conscious) audience engagement in the suppression of the subversive textual "inside." All of this turns on Althusser's familiar notion that "*individuals are always-already subjects*," hailed or "interpellated," and thus "subjected," by the ruling ideology even before they are born. Thus the "imaginary relationship of individuals to the real conditions of existence" is a distortion imposed on the subject from without, and not—as I would have it—the result of a denial by the individual of elements that conflict with the dominant, preferred conception of the world. Althusser's "individual" lives in an illusion of freedom but is in fact the passive subject of a distorting ideology; mine, on the other hand, is actively engaged in what I take to be a definitively cultural variety of self-deception.[24]

A version of Althusser's distinction between the "real" and the "imaginary" seems to turn up in the work of Pierre Macherey, who argues that the surface order of literature

> is merely an imagined order, projected on to disorder, the fictive resolution of ideological conflicts, a resolution so precarious that it is obvious in the very letter of the text where incoherence and incompleteness burst forth. It is no longer a question of defects but of indispensable informers. This distance which separates the work from the ideology which it transforms is rediscovered in the very letter of the work: it is fissured, unmade even in its making. . . . The disorder that permeates the work is related to the disorder of ideology (which cannot be organised as a system). The work derives its form from this incompleteness which enables us to identify the active presence of a conflict at its borders.[25]

As applied to the work of Jules Verne, this approach leads to the discovery that the ostensibly futuristic Captain Nemo is in fact modelled on Robinson Crusoe. Such a glaring inconsistency confirms for Macherey that "bourgeois ideology has become incapable of thinking and representing the future," and points, in turn, to the "contradictory" relation between Verne's "profoundly ideological notion . . . of labour and conquest" and "the historical reality which it recuperates." "Real labour," he goes on, "is alienated, perfect conquest is inevitably constrained by the conditions of former colonisation. These are the real limits of bourgeois ideology: but this ideology is emphatically not internally contradictory; for that would presuppose that it gave a complete description of reality, that it ceased to be an ideology, whereas it is precisely its insufficiencies, its incompleteness, which guarantee its flawed coherence."[26]

Macherey's apparent uncertainty about the coherence (or incoherence) of ideology tends at least to confirm that he is primarily concerned with the contradictions between bourgeois ideology, as it is represented in literature, and the historical reality which the text distorts.[27] The emphasis here is of course reminiscent of Althusser. But Macherey's eye for oppositions within the text, and his sense of the literary work as an utterance standing in place of "other things *which must not be said*," are key points of intersection between his thinking and my own. While it is true that Macherey locates "the forbidden term" outside the text (while I find it at large within it),[28] his insistence that "its absence is unacknowledged" is consonant with my view of the denial of denial in bad faith.

The notion, shared by Althusser and Macherey, that ideology conceals the "real" world beneath an imposed, "imaginary" veneer stands in contrast to Jameson's model for mass culture, in which a utopian trace is overlaid by manipulative distortion.[29] The results of my own study strongly suggest a third perspective, one that characterizes the surface as an evasive fabrication and the submerged content as a relatively subversive construction with an evident foundation in reality. Because I emphasize the role of the audience in the foregrounding—and therefore in the formation—of the textual surface, I am not inclined to dismiss that surface as a manipulative "bribe." The audience is similarly involved in the evasion of the repressed content, that more faithful construction of reality whose submerged presence is an essential ingredient in the authority of the text. Properly observed and understood, this specifically cultural pattern of evasive maneuvering between contrary constructions of reality gives us a window on history as it shapes itself in the popular imagination.

5

In good part because of his sense of the relationship between literature and reality, Terry Eagleton's work speaks in useful ways to the dynamics of the texts assembled here. "Narrative," he argues, "far from constituting some ruling-class conspiracy, is a valid and ineradicable mode of all human experience. More precisely, it is the very form of the ideological; and since the ideological will not disappear with the dismantling of class-society, neither will narrative." Eagleton goes on to insist that "we cannot think, act, or desire except in narrative; it is by narrative that the subject constructs that 'sutured' chain of signifiers which grants its true condition of division sufficient 'imaginary' coherence to enable it to act."[30] This is not to suggest that the constructed world is an utter fabrication. While "the real is by necessity empirically imperceptible," the ideology that stands in its place "so produces and constructs the real as to cast the shadow of its absence over the perception of its presence." Thus history appears in the literary text, as it does in all narrative, "precisely *as ideology*, as a presence determined and distorted by its measurable absences."[31]

This is apposite both because of its emphasis on telling omissions, and because of its insistence on an oblique linkage between the text and a history that is as real as it is empirically inaccessible in any "pure" form. The linkage is doubly oblique in literature, Eagleton continues, because "the literary text does not *take* history as its object, even when (as with 'historical' fiction) it believes itself to do so." This apparent freedom from the contingencies of the real means in fact that literature operates at two removes from the reality that the intervening ideological matrix obliquely represents. Literature is the fictional representation of the ideological representation of the real. This is an attenuated relation to history, but it is not an illusory one. For if, as Eagleton argues, the text "distantiates history, it is not because it transmutes it to fantasy, shifting from one ontological gear to another, but because the significations it works into fiction are already representations of reality rather than reality itself."[32]

My version of Eagleton's textual ideology is more nearly "real" than his. As the Jim submerged in *Huckleberry Finn* or the Marian submerged in *Shane* reveal, the absences in these novels are filled by presences—plausible constructions of the historical real—just below the surface. My texts do not exclude or hopelessly distort history; rather, they represent it even as they maneuver to conceal it. This major difference in emphasis notwithstanding, Eagleton's scheme runs closely parallel to my own, especially in its tripartite division between history, which is "outside" the text and accessible only in mediated form; ideology, the first-level representation of the historical real; and the ideology of the text, the emphatically "fictive" rendering of society's self-representations. Eagleton goes on to discuss fictions that "display variable degrees of internal conflict and disorder—a disorder produced by those displacements and mutations of ideology enforced upon the text by the necessity to arrive, in accordance with the laws of its aesthetic production, at a 'solution' to its problems."[33] As applied to *Huckleberry Finn*, this model reinforces my sense of a distinction between the submerged narrative of Jim's suffering in slavery (as it is dramatized in his conflicted relationship with Huck) and the surface rendering of the peculiar institution—with its emphasis on the love between Huck and Jim, and on the resolution of "the problem" in the "freeing" of Jim—as it appears within the novel, and in its enduring popular reception. I would make a similar distinction between the competing versions of family life, and of Marian's domestic role, in *Shane*.

But these applications serve to underscore another key difference between Eagleton's view and my own. While he argues that the text is esthetically driven, and proposes "to itself only such problems as it can resolve, or leave unresolved without radically interrogating the terms of its problematic,"[34] I point to the potently subversive representations within narrative, elements that are concealed and denied precisely because they resist resolution, esthetic or otherwise. In parallel fashion, while I share his inclination to highlight the "fictiveness" of literature, I do not find that this quality arises primarily out of the "text's lack of a real direct referent."[35] *Huckleberry Finn* is most conspicuously "fictive" in the closing, "humorous" chapters, where the increasingly desperate evasion of emergent revelations about slavery is manifest in manifold implausibilities. This subversive strain within the text, in which Huck's concealed feelings about Jim are explored and in which Jim's motives are at least glimpsed, registers a drift back toward the unbearable but irresistible real, and not merely a further, fictive elaboration upon a manageable "problem." The same may be said of Bob's persistent disclaimers in *Shane;* it is the very implausibility of his professions of ignorance that prompt us to look for the repressed but hardly resolved or resolvable issues that they conceal. Likewise the heightened artifice in the closing chapters of *The Last of the Mohicans* is an index to the resurgence of the novel's restless, unmanageable contradictions.

Thus in my popular novels an increase of artifice generally signals an increase in the strain of the narrative under the pressure of contradictions emergent from within its "ideology." A heightening of the "fictive" is the sign of an evasion of contradiction, of the refusal to acknowledge that the representation of the real is in some vital way unfaithful to the truth of its object. Slavery, or domestic life, or racial and sexual boundaries, these texts seem reluctantly to admit, are not as neatly and happily manageable as they may first appear. This is to reiterate that my texts represent, however evasively, real problems—problems with a manifest foundation in history and problems notable for their resistance to satisfactory resolution. It is also to emphasize that the *ideology* of the text, as I might use that term, is neither the surface nor the submerged representation of such problems but the often uneasy relationship between those levels. I say "often" because the relative ease or difficulty with which discord is "managed" varies quite considerably from text to text and from reader to reader. This is of course to insist upon the vital role of the audience in the formation of the ideology of the text, and to stress that this involvement entails an active part in the "management" of painful contradictions. The bad faith thus obliquely glimpsed is the manifestation of a widely shared cultural impulse to defend favored prepossessions about self and society from the revelation of their imperfect conformity to the real.

But it is of course crucial to reiterate that increased attention to concealment is in fact an indirect revelation; that evasion is simultaneously an oblique acknowledgment of that which is denied. In its relentless attention to what is "feminine" in Maud, *The Sea-Wolf* indirectly reveals an alternative persuasion about its heroine; just so, in its climactic celebration of marriage and domesticity, *The Virginian* offers us a glimpse of submerged resistance to the forward thrust of the narrative. And in the very freeing of Jim we are made witness to what will continue to enslave him. Thus it is the presence, not the absence, of major cultural contradictions that draws large audiences back to these texts. Nor can we plausibly argue that readers are completely blind to what, once observed, is so conspicuous and irresistible about these books. The contradictory strain is so central and persistent that we must feature it prominently in any attempt to account for popularity. At the same time, we must ask how it is that the vast majority of readers, including trained literary analysts, manage somehow to overlook the obvious in this way.

THEORETICAL POSTSCRIPT

6

There is at least part of an answer, I believe, in what I have defined as bad faith, the broadcast, recapitulating cycle of address and evasion of our departures—in this case our most embarrassing departures—from leading notions of what is right and just. These are failures that we cannot seem to witness fully or for long; yet they are too much a part of our world, and too potently challenging to our self-esteem, to be swept permanently from sight and mind. Popular representations engage us precisely because they facilitate this almost compulsive going back and forth. We are drawn to them not because they are free of discord, but rather because in seeming to contain it they must, perforce, reinvoke it. We can view this process from a different angle by pointing to the profoundly self-subversive strain in these popular fictions. Narratives like *Riders of the Purple Sage, The Sea-Wolf, Pudd'nhead Wilson,* and the others, I have argued, are not finally disposed to acquiesce in tidy concluding constructions. Nor, I would add, are we. In the audience, as in the text, the impulse to conceal answers an impulse to reveal, and vice versa.

This having it both ways—seeing and not seeing, grasping in consciousness only to repress—is not always pathological. As the play in a culture's often rigid structures, bad faith has the potential to allay inevitable tensions and to enhance equity. But the social problems represented in my popular texts are probably not well served by the process of evasion they at once dramatize and reinforce. To be sure, these novels are witness to an incomplete surrender to denial. The impulse to evade is here found in combination with an incapacity, even a refusal, to fully forget. But the "solutions" advanced in *The Last of the Mohicans, Shane,* and *Pudd'nhead Wilson* are affirmations of the status quo, and thus oblique acknowledgments of an unreadiness to envision significant change. Indeed, I have argued that this simultaneous drive and failure to confront grave wrong in *Huckleberry Finn* is an example of bad faith in its pathological phase. This is to reiterate, from another angle, my resistance to Terry Eagleton's view that texts propose to themselves only such problems as they can readily resolve. Richard Dyer makes the same claim, but with specific reference to musicals. Allowing that "entertainment" addresses itself "to real needs *created by society,*" he adds that it in fact represents only those needs "that *capitalism* proposes itself to deal with." Because "class, race and sexual caste are denied validity as problems by the dominant (bourgeois, white, male) ideology of society,"[36] these matters are not represented in show business. This may be the case. But it does not follow that class, race, and sexual caste are excluded from consideration in popular literature. To the contrary, they are centrally represented *as problems* in many of our most enduring popular texts. And this is so, I suggest, not because they have somehow slipped past the mechanisms of capitalist cultural censorship, but because—in the texts studied here, at least—the simultaneous betrayal and evasion of moral contradiction is the sine qua non of popularity. We are drawn back again and again because our bad faith evasions are always incomplete, because the refusal to acknowledge our deferred promises and compromised values is culturally part and parcel with the inability to eclipse them for long from sight and mind.

7

The concealments performed and permitted by popular literature would appear to have a partial foundation in the dynamics of culture itself, which arises out of and builds upon the denial of its own constructedness. The wide-ranging play of bad faith, I am suggesting, is analogous to and in a sense "authorized" by what James Clifford, following Nietzsche, calls the "lie of culture." It is because the individual "learns to lie," to acquiesce more or less completely in the "reality" of the world as given, that he or she is able "to communicate within the collective, partial fictions of cultural life."[37] I am inclined, as Clifford is, to make a potential virtue of this cultural necessity, and to regard as extreme the view that the "lie of culture" leads directly to the slippery slope of nihilism and the abyss. Indeed, Peter L. Berger and Thomas Luckmann argue quite persuasively that our ability to confer legitimacy on humanly constructed "symbolic universes" is the key to such sanity as we possess, and perhaps to our survival. "*All* social reality," they insist, "is precarious. *All* societies are constructions in the face of chaos. The constant possibility of anomic terror is actualized whenever the legitimations that obscure the precariousness are threatened or collapse."[38] In this view we have endured because we have denied the painful truth of our condition, accepted the sweeping "lie of culture" and then successfully concealed from ourselves that we have any part in the construction of "reality."

Other scholars have made the same point in somewhat different terms. Pierre Bourdieu argues that "the explanation agents may provide of their own practice, thanks to a quasi theoretical reflection on their practice, conceals, even from their own eyes, the true nature of their practical mastery, i.e., that it is *learned ignorance (docta ignorantia),* a mode of practical knowledge not comprising knowledge of its own principles." Bourdieu stresses that "the work of denial which is the source of social alchemy is, like magic, a collective undertaking." Accordingly, he gives special emphasis to the place of silence and diversion and camouflage and oversight in the legitimating of the established order.[39] Roy Wagner is equally inclined to highlight the element of denial in the construction of reality. Human beings are "very clever and elusive masquerade and disguise" artists. "We create nature," he reflects, "and tell ourselves stories about how nature creates us." Wagner describes the "invention of culture" as a dialectical process that involves a necessary "restriction of vision" or "masking" that shields culture bearers "from the essential relativism of all symbolic construction." Because our collective fictions grow thin with use, we are forever drifting toward "unmasking" and the abyss of "relativization." Consequently we are obliged to engage in the constant reinvention of culture—which is to say, in the constant denial of the chaos that lurks along the margins of consciousness.[40]

If it is true, as these scholars agree, that culture is conceived and sustained in the denial of encroaching anomie, then the persistence of more specifically focused evasions in our popular texts makes a special kind of sense. Fictions like *Huckleberry Finn* and *Shane* manage anomic terror by clearing a space for the construction of meaning in its place. At the same time that they tell this "lie of culture" with extraordinary authority, these texts also fill the space thus cleared with actions whose significance is almost always bound up with more specific evasions. These "levels" of denial are not always easily distinguished. But the performance of such double duty—summoning and then banishing the specters of the "lie of culture" and of the kindred, lesser lies that define our distinctive construction of reality—is undoubtedly a factor in the great popularity in these texts. Consider, in this light, the regularity with which our favorite books approach the brink of the abyss only in the end to lead us toward what appears to be higher, much safer ground. In the mass confusion of roles toward the end of *The Last of the Mohicans,* for example, or in the virtual submergence of Huck's identity in Tom's (toward the end of *Huckleberry Finn*), we glimpse, and then gratefully lose sight of, the sheer constructedness of our social realities. Just as their specific movements of bad faith always reveal what they subsequently conceal, so these texts characteristically betray, in bold relief, the more general arbitrariness that they so successfully deny.

Our sense that cultural constructions are necessary appears in a telling state of tension with our sense that culture is conceived in a lie. This habit of moralizing culture is to some extent the issue of the dominant Judeo-Christian element in our construction of the world, and of the related tendency to valorize the natural—which we equate with innocence, simplicity, sincerity, humility—in contrast to the artificial, the man-made, the corrupt. We have constructed reality in a way that disposes us to view reality construction, when it is glimpsed, with great suspicion. But I want to suggest that there is more than a reverence for Galilean simplicity at work here. The "lie of culture" also gets its bad name with us because we tend to conflate it with what we sense are the *unnecessary* lies in the world we have constructed for ourselves. We would be happier with the grand fiction of reality if our leading cultural fictions were less morally compromised in their evasions. Our uncertainties in this area are rarely drawn fully into consciousness—our most popular stories characteristically reveal dark truths only to conceal them again—but the traces of those revelations play along the margins of consciousness, drawing us back to our most favored stories, yet at the same time preserving in us the suspicion that those potent fictions—and all fictions, including the fiction of culture itself—are not merely constructions, but lies.

This general suspicion of all social constructions is, let me repeat, a misapprehension with a specific—and constructed—cultural foundation. I take support for this view from Clifford Geertz, who has noted with dismay our tendency to ideologize ideology, and has labored to rescue the term from ignominy. Passing over the "interest" theory of ideology, Geertz adopts a version of what he calls the "strain" theory, with its emphasis on the varieties of "malintegration" to be found in *all* systems of society and the self. "It is when neither a society's most general cultural orientations nor its most down-to-earth, 'pragmatic' ones suffice any longer to provide an adequate image of political process that ideologies begin to become crucial as sources of sociopolitical meanings and attitudes." Geertz highlights the political in the ideological, but he insists on a broad definition that makes room as well for the moral, economic, and aesthetic dimensions. Indeed, he assigns to ideology the task, for good and for ill, of establishing and defending patterns of belief and value.[41]

Geertz's position anticipates my own not only in many of its details but also in the general conception of ideology as a necessary and potentially very constructive human resource. Thus freed from its more familiar, much narrower associations, the term overlaps with my understanding of culture in its lowercase expression—as the sense made of race or slavery or gender in the novels I have studied. I emphasize, where Geertz does not, the element of denial in the construction of meaning; but we agree that ideology enables humans to make meaning when and where it is perceived to be wanting. We agree as well in construing culture in its broadest terms as this meaning-making capacity in its most direct and primary expression. "The tool-making, laughing, or lying animal, man," according to Geertz, "is also the incomplete—or, more accurately, self-completing—animal. The agent of his own realization, he creates out of his general capacity for the construction of symbolic models the specific capacities that define him."[42] Culture is thus "the machinery individuals and groups of individuals employ to orient themselves in a world otherwise opaque."[43] But, let me reiterate, ideology is also for Geertz a precious stay against confusion. "It is a loss of orientation," he declares, "that most directly gives rise to ideological activity."[44] Culture, it appears, is a broader, more fundamental, more permanent form of ideology. It is the foundation, the bedrock of assumptions without which ideology could not take rise. Again I would merely emphasize that denial—specifically, the denial of the world's essential opaqueness—is a key element in that world-constructing capacity. Without it, we could never eclipse from consciousness the obdurate resistance of reality to our sensible designs.

I have prodded this structural and functional homology into view because it rather neatly prefigures the parallel I have drawn between uppercase Culture, which enables our acquiescence in reality as we find it, and lowercase culture, our more specific constructions of the personal and social real. I highlight this distinction because it opens the way to a fuller understanding of our reasons for returning to books like *The Last of the Mohicans, Huckleberry Finn, Shane,* and the others. Popular taste is no doubt a complicated cultural phenomenon about which we have much to learn. But novels win large and enduring audiences, I want to suggest, because they at once challenge and reinforce our sense of the world's reality, and our confidence in the legitimacy of the major personal and social constructions that fill that reality. Both of these dispositions to the world are fragile, in part because both are based on conspicuous evasions, and in part because if they are mutually reinforcing, they are also rather complexly synergistic in their tendencies to collapse. But of course it is the very precariousness of our credulity that prompts us, and even all but obliges us, to return to these familiar texts. Popularity is the measure of the success with which a text leads us toward and away from a full reckoning with the "lie of culture" and the cognate bad faith of the constructions that it enables. Given too little denial, we retreat from an unbearable excess of our own reality; given too much, our need to manage the world, to reinvent it in terms of our preferred assumptions, is not permitted the free play that it requires.

Geertz's development of the notions of culture and ideology is also useful in its reminder that the indeterminacy of the real does not render it unreal. The world, he says, is "opaque"—emphatically present and visible, but obscure, unintelligible. The symbolic codes by which we confer meaning on that world, and thereby come to know it, bring light to a reality that is as phenomenally irresistible as it is unknowable in its own terms. But in seeming to penetrate the opaqueness of things as they are, our symbolic constructions simply interpose a lucid barrier between us and the unknown. They do not in fact penetrate the obscurity; rather, they bury it in light, and at the same time obscure the fact of what they have done. Thus the knowledge effect is no more or less than the denial of denial—a necessary, world-creating and world-sustaining model for all lesser varieties of bad faith.[45] In its more extreme forms, this profound evasive urge tends, on one side, toward the complete naturalization of the symbolic, and, on the other, toward the total eclipse of the world in an aestheticized or horrified contemplation of arbitrary fictional designs. More commonly, it drives that relentless push-pull in consciousness between what we want (indeed, need) to know, and the darker, less tractable stuff that we cannot quite press out of sight and mind.

If culture and ideology are alike in their essential constructedness, then they are alike as well in requiring of us that we obscure from ourselves the fundamental concealment that they perform. It must be emphasized that this denial of denial at the very heart of the meaning-making enterprise is also at the root of much of the paradox and contradiction that figure so prominently in studies of our symbolic constructions. Culture and ideology have their being in doubleness; they are in the business of having things both ways. Quite evidently, individuals and groups vary in the degree to which they practice this inherent duplicity. There is obvious variety as well in the ways in which humans have adapted this "play" to constructive ends or turned it instead against themselves and others. But the doubleness, the reciprocal deception of self and other and the consequent paradox and contradiction, are always already with us.

8

This book, and *In Bad Faith* before it, are attempts to trace the specific American trajectory of this doubleness at the core of all culture. In observing our popular literary self-constructions, I have learned a great deal from both Marxist and deconstructionist arguments; but, it must be obvious by now, I have found neither completely satisfying. There are more or less healthy cultures, and more or less sick ones, but I think none has fallen, thanks to capitalism (or any other "cause"), from innocence into ideology. With D. A. Miller, I want to "stress the positivity of contradiction, which, far from always marking the fissure of a social formation, may rather be one of the joints whereby such a formation is articulated." But to argue that all ideology, like all signification, is constructed and therefore inherently ambiguous, is not, as I have already suggested, necessarily to flirt with the void. It is instead to be reminded that our symbolic structures develop in particular contexts, in specific historical circumstances that anchor the play of ambiguity to local, interested frames of reference. "Undecidability," as Miller puts it, "must always be the undecidability of *something in particular*."[46]

CHAPTER 5

In the popular texts that I have analyzed, this "something in particular" is racial prejudice, slavery, and varieties of sexual inequality. Time and again it is to these issues that we return, it is around these issues that paradox and contradiction gather. It is here, these novels seem obliquely to declare, that we are most inclined to want to have things both ways. I emphasize the "we" in order to reiterate that bad faith is as much the responsibility of the audience as it is of the text and the author. If we are taken in, we are also perpetually ready to be deceived. Mark Twain is nowhere more profoundly one of us than in his inability to confront fully what he could not finally forget about race-slavery. *Huckleberry Finn* speaks for us, just as it speaks for him, because it represents the most painful chapter in our history in a way that is responsive to the pressure of our cultural prepossessions. A text achieves popularity, in this view, because it represents major social issues in ways that anticipate the culture's need to be deceived. Thus *Shane* reveals what we would agree on principle to be the injustice of Marian's dilemma, but it does so in a way that readily facilitates the evasion of that insight, with its numerous awkward implications. This is not to suggest that Mark Twain and Jack Schaefer are willful manipulators, or that we are willful collaborators in these evasions. Rather, I believe that we join these writers and their novels in the mainstream of the culture, where bad faith—the seeing and not seeing of the unbearable/unforgettable, and the denial of denial—plays out, in local terms, the larger "lie of culture." Nor is this to neutralize the moral weight of these evasions in an argument from necessity. Doubleness may be endemic to culture, but these particular varieties of doubleness are not. Evidently enough, we have alternatives. But it is not, on the other side, to suggest that we are somehow extraordinary or unnatural in our habits of bad faith. Consciousness is threatened on every side with the encroachment of anomie. Little wonder that consciousness denies the unbearable truth of its condition. Little wonder in turn that consciousness shrinks from the contradictions that arise, willy-nilly, from the midst of its constructions. We are free, perhaps, to make and to remake our world. As our popular classics make clear, the evasive urge is in tension with resistance to denial, and with an impulse to address those vital truths we retreat from. It is surely within us to look more squarely at texts such as these, and at the enduring problems they strain to express. But we are no freer in this enterprise than we can bear to be; and that, I suspect, is not as free as we think we ought to be. We must resist denial, even in this.

9

In rounding to a close on these theoretical reflections, I am brought back to an acknowledgment of my large indebtedness to the work of Stephen Greenblatt. I am everywhere attentive to his analysis of "the process whereby subversive insights are generated in the midst of apparently orthodox texts and simultaneously contained by those texts."[47] Greenblatt powerfully reinforces my sense that this is a dialectical process, a ceaseless transformational play back and forth between social and literary constructions. The impulse here is to dramatically narrow the gap between art and society, and to highlight their dynamic, always interested negotiations with each other. Greenblatt emphasizes that this ongoing cultural interplay, which profoundly informs the individual's sense of the wholeness and intelligibility of the "real," is at the same time the source of no little ambiguity and contradiction. Such concealed doubleness is inherently a feature of all reality constructions, but it is also, in its more "local" manifestations, the servant of "specific, institutional interests." Greenblatt acknowledges that signifiers play, and he gives capitalism its day, but the deeper, more enduring source of doubleness, he insists, is the subtly self-serving play of power.[48]

The ambiguous ways and means of power are the subject of Greenblatt's well-known essay, "Invisible Bullets: Renaissance Authority and Its Subversion." The argument proceeds from the observation that the imposition of the Christian order upon the "savages" of the New World had the effect of exposing the arbitrariness of leading articles of that conquering faith. But this marked and unsettling subversive tendency was at the same time "contained" by the system that it appeared to threaten. Indeed, Greenblatt goes on to argue that the colonial power structure produced its own subversion in order that it might build upon it. "The radical undermining of Christian order," he finds, "is not the negative limit but the positive condition for the establishment of that order."[49]

The question follows, of course, why Renaissance authority should have permitted, and even fostered, this exposure of its deeply Machiavellian methods. "The answer," Greenblatt reflects, "may be in part that power, even in a colonial situation, is not perfectly monolithic and hence may encounter and record in one of its functions materials that can threaten another of its functions; in part that power thrives on vigilance, and human beings are vigilant if they sense a threat; in part that power defines itself in relation to such threats or simply to that which is not identical with it." Finally, and in the greatest detail, he declares that "the simple operation of any systematic order . . . will inevitably run the risk of exposing its own limitations, even (or perhaps especially) as it asserts its underlying moral principle."[50]

Greenblatt's central proposition, that authority has "as its positive condition the constant production of its own radical subversion and the powerful containment of that subversion,"[51] applies to my texts nearly as well as it does to his. We are both interested in art forms that tell and untell, reveal only to conceal, the same unsettling story. We agree that this distinctive feature in our texts is not the result of conscious authorial intention, but appears as part of a complex process of circulation and exchange in which the artist and artifact and audience renegotiate and confirm their ties to the forces that authorize their construction of reality.[52] Greenblatt argues quite persuasively, for example, that Elizabethan audiences were constantly subjected to theatrical strategies for "arousing and manipulating anxiety," strategies with clear analogues in the social and political realm, which were "brought to a kind of perfection in Shakespeare." Anxiety in the "real" world had its most immediate source in copious, vivid signs of potently coercive political authority. Shakespeare's plays render these same signs in a way designed to give pleasure and thereby win continued audience patronage. The key to success in this simultaneously mimetic and commercial enterprise, Greenblatt observes, is "bound up with the marking out of theatrical anxiety as represented anxiety—not wholly real, either in the characters onstage or in the audience." Thus "the aesthetic space—or, more accurately, the commercial space of the theatrical joint-stock company—is constituted by the simultaneous appropriation of and swerving from the discourse of power."[53]

Along with numerous similarities, there are inevitable differences in emphasis to be observed here. Greenblatt does not align his analysis of literary doubleness, as I do, with a larger, informing "lie of culture." When it is framed in this way, power may be seen to express itself first in the authorization of meaning, in that denial of the denial of anomie that empowers the individual in culture to make sense of—to construct, or reconstruct—the world. Literary authority, I have argued, is closely bound up with the central role of literature in the formation and reinforcement of the all-informing assumption that the world is intelligible. Nor does Greenblatt stress, as I think we must, the extent to which social and political power are an embarrassment in a Judeo-Christian cultural setting. That we find Machiavelli's ideas both persuasive and abrasive is an index to our very mingled perspective on secular power. To the very considerable degree that they are Christian in origin, our notions of freedom and justice, and our esteem for innocence, and for humility in the face of mystery, will fall into some measure of conflict with virtually all manifestations of social and political authority. The marked tendency toward self-subversion in literature has a partial foundation, I believe, in deeply divided affiliations and loyalties along this conflicted border. And it is for this reason that literary self-subversion is likely to be "most intense," in Greenblatt's words, "when the moral value of a particular form of power is not merely assumed but explained."[54]

This latter variation in emphasis brings us back to the place of moral concerns in the dynamics of representation. Greenblatt recognizes such concerns, but he does not feature them centrally in his analysis. In my readings, on the other hand, the preeminence of the notion of bad faith is conspicuous. This very marked critical departure has its foundation in the differences between the cultural contexts from which our texts emerge. Greenblatt shows that the manipulation of audience anxiety in the Renaissance theater had its analogue in the strategies of social and political control wielded by authoritarian Tudor and Stuart monarchs. Shakespeare converted audience anxiety to the purposes of pleasure, but his manipulative theatrical technique was nonetheless intimately bound up with coercive social practices. Indeed, the Globe was hardly more theatrical than the government. Political power was dramatized for the Elizabethans in regular encounters with the awesome spectacle of royal grandeur, and with the evidence, draped on the city gates, of sudden, brutal violence. Thus the stage operated in the shadow of the scaffold; even in its pleasure the audience acknowledged the sway of towering, punishing authority.

This heavy dose of coercive subjection in Elizabethan theatrical and social practice contrasts with the experience of the modern consumer of culture. The pleasure of the Shakespearean audience, as described by Greenblatt, was to some extent the issue of the dramatic subversion of authority. Pleasure came with a sigh of relief at the revelation that represented power was just that—represented, a fictional construction. But the source of anxiety did not disappear; rather, it was brought by the play into a softer, happier light. The modern audience, by contrast, takes its representations not so much on the stage as in novels and on television. The point of vantage is more remote, cooler, and power is represented, when it appears, either as a force for good on the side of the observer or as the possession of an evil or irrelevant other. But if represented power is not a source of anxiety for most American readers or viewers, then guilt—the emergent sense of individual moral responsibility for represented, socially and politically authorized departures from public notions of the good and the just—is. Our anxiety is part and parcel with a sense of complicity in the inherent inequities and tragic miscarriages and abuses of power. Shane does not threaten us with punishment, as the Shakespearean heroes seem to have threatened their first audiences. But the good in Shane's violence may prompt us to reflect anxiously on the authorized violence in our world, a violence often rooted in varieties of inequality. And in Shane's apparently fair-minded dealings with Marian we may also catch a glimpse, though probably not a conscious one, of the inequities with which she must contend, and even the extent to which that injustice is bound up with the ideal of male heroism embodied in the cowboy. But the anxiety that accompanies those intimations is readily dissipated in the overriding sense that violence is necessary to peace and progress, and that Marian's problems are as manifestly her own fault as her triumphs are properly partial ones.

The popular American texts I have studied are written for an audience of empowered participants in the social and political process. Most of the members in this audience, unlike the patrons of the Globe, perceive themselves as enfranchised, morally responsible actors in, not the merely passive subjects of, the world that unfolds before them. Thus their anxiety arises out of a feeling of inner complicity with power, and not from the spectacle of its threatening encroachment from without.[55] Concomitantly, their pleasure results not from the revelation of the constructedness of power but from the concealment of its injustices. It is not what the audience sees, but what it contrives not to see, that provides the relief; and it is relief from the anxiety arising out of guilt, and not out of fear, that contributes to the experience of pleasure. It follows that the Renaissance audience was relatively much less active than its modern counterpart in the actual construction of the meaning that it took away from its experience. Shakespeare's audience endured a happy subjection to the dramatic subversion of power; the audience that I have in mind participates with the text, and with its author/narrator, in the active evasion of departures from justice.

10

But concealment implies an accompanying revelation; evasions in literature, or in the literary response, are the correlative to the presence of something offensive to consciousness. The popular text labors to restore our moral equanimity, even as it upsets it. At the same time that it dramatizes the destruction of indigenous peoples and the contradictions of racial and sexual prejudice, *The Last of the Mohicans* enlists our acquiescence in a vague sense of their inevitability. *Riders of the Purple Sage, The Virginian, The Sea-Wolf,* and *Shane* at once subvert and reconstruct the conventions of American heroism. Consider, finally, the example of Roxy, the beautiful slave who in *Pudd'nhead Wilson* switches the places of her own son and the virtually identical son of her master, thus sparing one child what she inflicts on the other. Over time Roxy comes to accept "the fiction created by herself," that her son

> was become her master; the necessity of recognizing this relation outwardly and of perfecting herself in the forms required to express the recognition, had moved her to such diligence and faithfulness in practicing these forms that this exercise soon concreted itself into habit; it became automatic and unconscious; then a natural result followed: deceptions intended solely for others gradually grew practically into self-deceptions as well; the mock reverence became real reverence, the

CHAPTER 5

mock obsequiousness real obesquiousness, the mock homage real homage; the little counterfeit rift of separation between imitation-slave and imitation-master widened and widened, and became an abyss, and a very real one—and on one side of it stood Roxy, the dupe of her own deceptions, and on the other stood her child, no longer a usurper to her, but her accepted and recognized master.[56]

Roxy's act is profoundly subversive of the slave system, and of the more enduring white power structure. The subversion only begins with the switching of the children; it extends to the revelation that the carefully guarded racial boundaries defining the social and political relations of power are in fact highly permeable. Thus without really recognizing what she has done, Roxy reveals that the ideology of racial difference and white supremacy is an arbitrary, coercive, morally corrupt, and contradictory social construction.

Roxy's condition as slave does not exempt her from the contamination that comes from participation in this cruel "fiction." The bad faith of the masters involves the concealment of a palpable evil (slavery) in the fiction of an implausible good (the benefits of enslavement). Roxy's bad faith is less comprehensive to the extent that the freeing of her son is an undeniable good. But to save her baby she must take a long step into the heartless world of the masters; she must enslave a child to free one, and ruin a life to save one. Though her crime is at least partially redeemed by the extremity of her circumstances, Roxy is no more able to accept the cruelty of her act than her masters are able to accept the greater cruelty of theirs. Thus it is a very real, if entirely unacknowledged, function of her deliberate fictionalizing to conceal from herself the awful truth of what she has done.

In her own evasion of the unbearable truth, Roxy enacts a subversive parody of the bad faith of the social system in which she operates and, indeed, of the fiction-making system in which she is represented. For if *Pudd'nhead Wilson* tells a story that challenges our sense of moral equanimity, it also eases the way to its restoration. The denouement centers on the unravelling of a related but effectively distracting mystery plot whose solution returns the community to the complacent bad faith of the status quo ante. Roxy's role in the switching of the children is revealed, but the clear implications of her action for the larger system are never broached. At the same time, the text offers no consistent resistance to the inference that her actions serve to confirm the inferior moral status assigned to her by the dominant culture.

As a result the novel seems committed to the suppression of its strong subversive impulse. The available evidence strongly suggests that Mark Twain composed and revised and published *Pudd'nhead Wilson* without any awareness of the complex evasion that his fiction at once dramatized and enacted. But having argued quite persuasively that Mark Twain was imperfectly the master of his materials, Hershel Parker is surely wrong to insist that all attempts to make critical sense of *Pudd'nhead Wilson* must founder on the fundamental incoherence of the text.[57] Geared as they are to the novel's concealment of its subversive revelations, the anomalies and contradictions are meaningfully distorted testimony to the pervasive influence of bad faith. There is potent sense to the story's disorder. Just so, there is clear evidence of bad faith in Mark Twain's apparent belief that he had written a fast-paced murder mystery and not a penetrating indictment of race-slavery. Most of his readers have been inclined to agree with him. Indeed, it is the all-important key to the cultural authority of *Pudd'nhead Wilson* that it enables the retreat to an illusion of resolution when, in fact, the main business of the narrative has simply been pushed from sight and mind. To surrender in this way to the novel's drift is to recapitulate the bad faith evasion that *Pudd'nhead Wilson* at once commits and dramatizes. It is to miss the point, and thus, in a sense, to remain part of it.

NOTES

INTRODUCTION

1. For a much fuller elaboration, see my *In Bad Faith: The Dynamics of Deception in Mark Twain's America* (Cambridge: Harvard University Press, 1986).

2. Zane Grey's diary for 1 October 1905, as quoted by Carlton Jackson in *Zane Grey*, rev. ed. (Boston: Twayne, 1989), 12. On Grey's popularity, see Jackson, *Zane Grey*, 128–30, 140–42; and James D. Hart, *The Popular Book* (Berkeley and Los Angeles: University of California Press, 1963), 218–19.

3. Wayne Ude, "Forging an American Style: The Romance-Novel and Magical Realism as Response to the Frontier and Wilderness Experiences," in *The Frontier Experience and the American Dream*, ed. David Mogen et al. (College Station: Texas A & M University Press, 1989), 55–56. Northrup Frye observes that "the romance is nearest of all literary forms to the wish-fulfillment dream" (*Anatomy of Criticism* [New York: Atheneum, 1967], 186).

4. Jane Thompkins, "West of Everything," *South Atlantic Quarterly* 86 (1987): 370–71, 375, 367.

5. Ibid., 371.

6. Zane Grey, *Riders of the Purple Sage* (New York: Grosset & Dunlap, 1940), 39. Hereafter references to this edition will be cited parenthetically in the body of the text.

7. Grey, "My Own Life," in *Zane Grey: The Man and His Work* (New York: Harper & Brothers, 1928), 19.

8. William Bloodworth, "Zane Grey's Western Eroticism," *South Dakota Review* 23 (1985): 6. See also John D. Nesbitt, "Uncertain Sex in the Sagebrush," *South Dakota Review* 23 (1985): 15–27; Tompkins, Introduction to *Riders of the Purple Sage*, by Grey (New York: Penguin, 1990), who speculates that "Grey can't even let himself know that sex is what he is portraying" (xvii); and T. K. Whipple, who long ago observed (*Study Out the Land* [Berkeley and Los An-

geles: University of California Press, 1943], 240) that "in Zane Grey's conception of human nature nothing is more curious than his view of sex."

9. Tompkins, Introduction to *Riders of the Purple Sage*, by Grey, observes that Jane's "self-deception . . . in her treatment of Lassiter" is the "source" of Grey's "ambivalence toward her" (xxi).

10. Bloodworth, "Zane Grey's Western Eroticism," 8–9. "Apparently, Grey wanted to deal with adult topics," speculates Nesbitt ("Uncertain Sex in the Sagebrush," 26), "but he seems to have been peculiarly uncertain about how to deal with it in his fiction."

11. Whipple, *Study Out the Land*, 22.

12. Grey, "What the Open Means to Me," in *Zane Grey*, 36–37, 42.

CHAPTER 1   THE LAST OF THE MOHICANS

1. Michael Paul Rogin, *Fathers and Children: Andrew Jackson and the Subjugation of the American Indian* (New York: Knopf, 1975), 4.

2. Ibid., 6–9, 246–48, 243.

3. George Sand, *Autour de la Table*, as quoted by D. B. Wood, in *Fenimore Cooper: The Critical Heritage*, ed. George Dekker and John P. McWilliams (London: Routledge & Kegan Paul, 1973), 268. I am guided in remarks on Cooper's knowledge of contemporary Indian policy by James Franklin Beard's excellent Historical Introduction to *The Last of the Mohicans: A Narrative of 1757* (Albany, N.Y.: State University of New York Press, 1983).

4. James Fenimore Cooper, *Notions of the Americans: Picked up by a Travelling Bachelor*, (London: Henry Colburn, 1828), 2: 378.

5. Beard, Historical Introduction to *The Last of the Mohicans*, xxix.

6. Cooper, *Notions*, 2: 369, 378.

7. Richard Drinnon, *Facing West: The Metaphysics of Indian-Hating and Empire-Building* (Minneapolis: University of Minnesota Press, 1980), 162–63. John P. McWilliams, Jr. defines the problem in clearly related terms. See his *Political Justice in a Republic: James Fenimore Cooper's America* (Berkeley and Los Angeles: University of California Press, 1972), 244.

8. Cooper, *The Last of the Mohicans*, 197, 229, 112. Hereafter references to this (State University of New York) edition will be cited parenthetically in the text.

9. See the relevant section of Wood, *Fenimore Cooper: The Critical Heritage*.

10. Rogin, *Fathers and Children*, 4.

11. Ibid., 171, 247–48.

12. Drinnon, *Facing West*, 95–98.

13. James D. Wallace, *Early Cooper and His Audience* (New York: Columbia University Press, 1986), 18.

14. Leslie Fielder, *Love and Death in the American Novel* (New York: Criterion Books, 1960), 191.

15. McWilliams, *Political Justice in a Republic*, 240–41.

16. Roy Harvey Pearce, *The Savages of America: A Study of the Indian and the Idea of Civilization*, rev. ed. (Baltimore: Johns Hopkins University Press, 1965), 212, 232, 210.

17. Beard, Historical Introduction to *The Last of the Mohicans*, xxxi.

18. On Providence, see 116, where it informs Natty's resignation, and 257, where he confuses it with good luck. For variations on a definition of Heaven, see 315, 343, 344, 347, and 349.

19. Jane Tompkins, *Sensational Designs* (London: Oxford University Press, 1985), 109, 117, 118.

20. Wayne Franklin, *The New World of James Fenimore Cooper* (Chicago: University of Chicago Press, 1982), 238–40.

21. Thomas Philbrick, "*The Last of the Mohicans* and the Sounds of Discord," *American Literature* 43 (1971), 25–27.

22. Tompkins, *Sensational Designs*, 113: "Just as the human figures in Cooper's frontier fiction have the static quality of integers in a mathematical equation because they stand for fixed values in a system of value, so the plot has an air of artificiality and contrivance because it, too, answers the requirements of an abstract design." On 103 Tompkins describes *The Last of the Mohicans* as "social criticism written in an allegorical mode."

23. W. H. Gardiner, *North American Review* 23 (July 1826); in Dekker and McWilliams, *Fenimore Cooper: The Critical Heritage*, 117.

24. Tompkins, *Sensational Designs*, 113.

25. Ibid., 106. The rigidity of Tompkins's analysis tends to blind her to the psychological complexity of Cooper's characters, and to the novel's pervasive ambiguities.

26. Unsigned review, *New-York Review and Atheneum* 2 (March 1826); in Dekker and McWilliams, *Fenimore Cooper: The Critical Heritage*, 90.

27. Fielder, *Love and Death*, 182.

28. George Dekker, *James Fenimore Cooper: The American Scott* (New York: Barnes & Noble, 1967), 74–75.

29. Donald Davie, *The Heyday of Sir Walter Scott* (New York: Barnes & Noble, 1967), 109–10.

30. Davie argues that "the full-dress elegiac spectacle at the end of the book, the funeral for the last Mohican, Uncas, rings very hollow indeed" (*The Heyday*, 111). Cf. Philbrick's version of the same point, in "Sounds of Discord," 27.

31. Unsigned review, *New-York Review and Atheneum* 2 (March 1826); in Dekker and McWilliams, *Fenimore Cooper: The Critical Heritage*, 92–93.

32. Gardiner, *North American Review* 23 (July 1826); in Dekker and McWilliams, *Fenimore Cooper: The Critical Heritage*, 110–11.

33. Unsigned review, *United States Literary Gazette* 4 (May 1826); in Dekker and McWilliams, *Fenimore Cooper: The Critical Heritage*, 100.

34. Beard, ed., *The Letters and Journals of James Fenimore Cooper* (Cambridge: Harvard University Press, 1960), 1: xxxi.

35. "The true theatre of a demagogue," Cooper argues, "is a democracy." See his long, passionate chapter "On Demagogues" in his *The American Democrat* (1838; reprint, New York: Vintage, 1956), 96–102.

36. Tompkins, *Sensational Designs*, 99.

CHAPTER 2 THE VIRGINIAN

1. Owen Wister, *The Virginian* (New York: Pocket Books, 1956), 364. Hereafter page references to this edition will be cited parenthetically in the text.

2. For a much fuller elaboration of the national "program" embodied in the hero of *The Virginian*, see my article, "The Roosevelt-Wister Connection: Some Notes on the West and the Uses of History," *Western American Literature* 14 (1979): 95–114. John J. Murphy's essay, "The Virginian and Antonia Shimerda: Different Sides of the Western Coin," in *Women and Western American Literature*, ed. Helen Winter Stauffer and Susan J. Rosowski (Troy, N.Y.: Whitson Publishing, 1982), 162–78, very usefully enlarges the background against which Wister's novel may be viewed.

3. Gary Scharnhorst, "The Virginian as a Founding Father," *Arizona Quarterly* 40 (1984): 240.

CHAPTER 3 THE SEA-WOLF

1. Clarice Stasz, "Androgyny in the Novels of Jack London," *Western American Literature* 11 (1976): 121–33; Joan D. Hedrick, *Solitary Comrade: Jack London and His Work* (Chapel Hill: University of North Carolina Press, 1982), 112–13; Susan Ward, "Social Philosophy as Best-Seller: Jack London's *The Sea-Wolf*," *Western American Literature* 17 (1983): 321–32.

2. Robert Forrey, "Male and Female in London's *The Sea-Wolf*," *Literature and Psychology* 24 (1974): 135–43; Jon Yoder, "Jack London as Wolf Barleycorn," *Western American Literature* 11 (1976): 103–19.

3. Charles N. Watson, Jr., "Sexual Conflict in *The Sea-Wolf*," *Western American Literature* 11 (1976): 243–44.

4. Watson, "Sexual Conflict," 247.

5. As cited by Franklin Walker, Afterword to *The Sea-Wolf* by Jack London (New York: New American Library, 1964), 345.

6. Walker, Afterword to *The Sea-Wolf*, 345.

7. Watson, *The Novels of Jack London, A Reappraisal* (Madison: University of Wisconsin Press, 1983), 77; John Perry, *Jack London, An American Myth* (Chicago: Nelson-Hall, 1981), 161–62; Forrey, "Male and Female," 141; Hedrick, *Solitary Comrade*, 131–32; Stasz, "Androgyny," 124; Ward, "Social Philosophy," 331.

8. Hedrick, *Solitary Comrade*, 43.

9. London, *The Sea-Wolf*, ed. Matthew J. Bruccoli (Boston: Houghton Mifflin, 1964), 204. Hereafter page references to this edition will be noted parenthetically in the text.

10. For a lively and very useful portrait of Jordan and his ideas, see Kevin Starr's *Americans and the California Dream, 1850–1915* (New York: Oxford University Press, 1973), 307–44. Starr offers specific evidence of London's close attention to some of Jordan's leading ideas.

11. The same failure of precision occurs on the other occasions when Humphrey uses "terror" to describe Maud's reactions to Larsen; see 164 and 215.

12. Forrey, "Male and Female," 141.

13. Although Forrey goes on to add that Humphrey's homosexual desires "are clearly suspect" and that "one of the aims of the plot seems to be to purge Van Weyden of them" (141), he fails to recognize that such suspicions and corrective ambitions as surface in *The Sea-Wolf* are as intimately tied to the narrator's psychological organization as the homoerotic impulses to which they are addressed. It is Humphrey's manner of telling the story, and not "the plot," that betrays his attraction to Larsen, *and* his inability to consciously confront that suspicious attraction, *and* the ways and means of putting that attraction out of mind.

14. Maud's closest call with self-betrayal occurs when Humphrey's masculine bravado prompts him to announce, "I am capable of doing anything these days" (221). Maud succeeds in temporarily disguising her mirth, but her companion's foolishness is so invincible that she is finally incapable of controlling herself. Humphrey sees and rather dimly acknowledges the joke, but then gets so would up in his own theorizing that he emerges virtually unscathed. As usual, Humphrey's vanity is Maud's best ally.

15. London, *The Sea-Wolf*, 195, 233.

16. "Sexual Conflict," 246. Watson adds, "Not until Wolf is dying and powerless can Humphrey finally get his mast raised, and only after Wolf's death are Humphrey and Maud permitted their first passionate kiss" (246).

17. For a full and plausible analysis of London's neurotic need to think of himself as "a superman, one of Nietzsche's blond beasts or the Anglo-Saxon hero of Social Darwinist fantasy," see Starr, *Americans and the California*

Dream, 210 ff. Joan London's observations on her father's "latent homosexuality" are also relevant here; see *Jack London and His Times* (Seattle: University of Washington Press, 1968), 259–60.

18. I refer, of course, to the excellent chapter on London in Starr, *Americans and the California Dream*.

CHAPTER 4   SHANE

1. Jack Schaefer, *Shane*, The Critical Edition, ed. James C. Work (Lincoln: University of Nebraska Press, 1984), 133. Hereafter pagination from this edition will be cited parenthetically in the text.

2. The available evidence suggests that Schaefer was largely unconscious of the subversive strain that runs through his novel. He acknowledges that in the years after the publication of *Shane* he became disenchanted with the cowboy's role in accelerating the spread of civilized decadence. But this was a mood that replaced the "innocent attitude" that he brought to his first and most famous book. Later, he acknowledges, he surrendered to "a deepening conviction that my species, taken as a whole as in objective view it should be, is more ignoble than noble, more contemptible than admirable" (Afterword to *Shane*, 425, 423). In view of the strong undercurrents of skepticism emergent from *Shane*, it appears that a surreptitious erosion of his "innocent attitude" had in fact already commenced at the time of the composition of that novel.

3. D. H. Lawrence, *Studies in Classic American Literature* (New York: Viking, 1961), 62–63.

4. Gerald Haslam, "Jack Schaefer," in *Shane*, 31.

5. Fred Erisman, "Growing Up with the American West: Fiction of Jack Schaefer," in *Shane*, 297.

6. Michael Cleary, "Jack Schaefer: The Evolution of Pessimism," in *Shane*, 323–24. Cf. also Work, "Settlement Waves and Coordinate Forces in *Shane*," in *Shane*, 307–18.

7. E. L. Doctorow, "False Documents," in *E. L. Doctorow: Essays and Conversations*, ed. Richard Trenner (Princeton, New Jersey: Ontario Review Press, 1983), 16.

8. Ibid., 26.

9. Doctorow, *Welcome to Hard Times* (New York: Bantam, 1975), 213.

CHAPTER 5   THEORETICAL POSTSCRIPT

1. *In Bad Faith* was published by the Harvard University Press in 1986. More recently, in my "The Characterization of Jim in *Huckleberry Finn*," *Nine-*

teenth-Century Literature 43 (1988): 361–91, and in "The Sense of Disorder in Pudd'nhead Wilson," in *Mark Twain's Pudd'nhead Wilson: Race, Conflict, and Culture*, ed. Susan Gillman and Forrest G. Robinson (Durham: Duke University Press, 1990), 22–45, I have applied the notion of bad faith in new ways.

2. The distinction between popular and mass culture is much debated these days, but without any clear resolution. For example, to insist, as many theorists are inclined to, that popular art arises "from the people," whereas mass art "is imposed from above," makes sense only as the corollary of an elaborate, highly problematic theory of history. See Tania Modleski, ed., *Studies in Entertainment: Critical Approaches to Mass Culture* (Bloomington: Indiana University Press, 1986), xi. Because none of the texts discussed here would seem to qualify as a "mass" production, I will steer clear of that label. By "popular" literature I mean to describe, simply, books that enjoy a large audience.

3. Stephen Greenblatt, "The Cultivation of Anxiety: King Lear and His Heirs," *Raritan* 2 (1982): 103.

4. Fredric Jameson, *The Political Unconscious* (Ithaca, New York: Cornell University Press, 1981), 82.

5. Jameson, *Marxism and Form* (Princeton, New Jersey: Princeton University Press, 1971), 404.

6. The influence of Levi-Strauss and, in turn, of Saussure, is often evident, if only by implication, in much of the commentary in this general vein. Levi-Strauss's penchant for binarism, and his sense that it is "the purpose of myth . . . to provide a logical model capable of overcoming a contradiction" ("The Structural Study of Myth," in *Structural Anthropology* [New York: Basic Books, 1963], 229), are shared by numerous more recent students of culture. Even among those critics who acknowledge a debt, however, there are rather marked differences in application. Compare, for example, Will Wright, who faults Levi-Strauss for being too exclusively cognitive in his analysis of myth (*Sixguns and Society: A Structural Study of the Western* [Berkeley and Los Angeles: University of California Press, 1975], 16 ff), with Fredric Jameson, who finds in Levi-Strauss the anticipation of his own view that "the production of aesthetic or narrative form is . . . an ideological act in its own right, with the function of inventing imaginary or formal 'solutions' to unresolvable social contradictions" (*The Political Unconscious*, 79).

7. For a fuller definition, see Robinson, *In Bad Faith*, 26–27, 111–14, 211–15.

8. John G. Cawelti, *Adventure, Mystery, and Romance: Formula Stories as Art and Popular Culture* (Chicago: University of Chicago Press, 1976), 13. In this passage, and in the one following, Cawelti is referring to the formulaic elements in popular literature.

9. Ibid., 36. This is not to deny that more or less completely univocal texts

exist. But I am persuaded that our enduring popular stories—the ones we return to, and that we read or recommend to our children—are generally more complex in their organization.

10. Will Wright joins Cawelti as a notable exception to this general tendency. Wright contrasts high art with myth (as it appears in such popular Westerns as *Shane*). In the former, he argues, "the desire is usually for complex, realistic characters in situations that challenge social attitudes," whereas "myth depends on simple and recognizable meanings that reinforce rather than challenge social understanding" (*Sixguns and Society*, 23). Wright's emphasis on the social constructedness of popular myth is everywhere salutary. And it is well to be reminded that he is engaged in the analysis of films, not novels. Still, the commitment to "simple and recognizable meanings" is a liability of his rather rigid structural approach. To be sure, Wright features binary oppositions; but they are so tidy and superficial that they tend to obscure deeper tensions and contradictions. In fact, and quite contrary to Wright's analysis, the classic movie version of *Shane* (1953) preserves a number of the tensions and subversive strains that I have observed in the novel.

11. Clifford Geertz, "Person, Time, and Conduct in Bali," in *Local Knowledge: Further Essays in Interpretive Anthropology* (New York: Basic Books, 1983), 406. Geertz stresses that in addition to "this sort of natural counterpoint there are also simple, unbridged discontinuities between certain major themes themselves" (407).

12. Geertz, "Deep Play: Notes on the Balinese Cockfight," in *The Interpretation of Cultures: Selected Essays* (New York: Basic Books, 1973), 448.

13. Norman N. Holland, *The Dynamics of Literary Response* (New York: Oxford University Press, 1968), 28, 104, 74.

14. Sigmund Freud, "Repression," in *Collected Papers* (New York: Basic Books, 1959), 4: 86.

15. Freud, *The Interpretation of Dreams* (New York: Basic Books, 1965), 194.

16. On secondary revision, see Freud, *The Interpretation of Dreams*, 550–61, 601–3. My highlighting of the actively evasive elements in the Freudian scheme runs parallel to Herbert Fingarette's emphasis in his very helpful volume on *Self-Deception* (London: Routledge & Kegan Paul, 1969), 129–32. In angling to avoid the paradox of knowing ignorance conventionally associated with self-deception, Fingarette shifts the focus from knowledge and "seeing" to consciousness itself, arguing that we "disavow" our unacceptable "engagements" in the world by refusing to spell them out. His philosophical definition of "self-deception" is too narrow—too divorced from complicating cultural and historical considerations—to be directly applicable here. Nonetheless, his summary and critique of major theories of self-deception (most notably those of Kierkegaard, Freud, and Sartre), and his development of a coherent, paradox-free alternative, are of great value.

17. Jameson, "Reification and Utopia in Mass Culture," *Social Text* 1 (1979): 141, 144. For more on the place of Utopian "incentives" in the manipulation of mass cultural audiences, see Jameson, *The Political Unconscious*, 287–93.

18. Jameson, *The Political Unconscious*, 79.

19. Jameson, "Reification and Utopia," 144.

20. "It does not take much reflection to see," Jameson argues, "that a process of compensatory exchange must be involved here, in which the henceforth manipulated viewer is offered specific gratifications in return for his or her consent to passivity. In other words, if the ideological function of mass culture is understood as a process whereby otherwise dangerous and protopolitical impulses are 'managed' and defused, rechanneled and offered spurious objects, then some preliminary step must also be theorized in which these same impulses—the raw material upon which the process works—are initially awakened within the very text that seeks to still them" (*The Political Unconscious*, 287). Cf. also "Reification and Utopia," 144–45.

21. Jameson, *The Political Unconscious*, 79.

22. Jameson, "Reification and Utopia," 147.

23. Althusser argues (in "Ideology and Ideological State Apparatuses") that ideological contradictions express "the effects of the clashes between the capitalist struggle and the proletarian class struggle." At another point he adds that contradiction may result from the appearance "of the remnants of former ruling classes" within the currently dominant ideology. In *Lenin and Philosophy*, trans. Ben Brewster (London: New Left Books, 1971), 142, 146.

24. Ibid., 159, 164.

25. Pierre Macherey, *A Theory of Literary Production*, trans. Geoffrey Wall (London: Routledge & Kegan Paul, 1978), 155. In his "A Letter on Art," Althusser acknowledges and endorses Macherey's views on the relations between art and ideology (in *Lenin and Philosophy*, 203).

26. Macherey, *A Theory of Literary Production*, 237–38.

27. Macherey goes on to add that his analysis is not "yet another new 'interpretation' of Verne's work, another translation, another commentary; on the contrary it is an explanation of the discords which connect the work to itself. These discords are not finally the direct reflection of an ideological contradiction, but the symptom of a historical opposition" (*A Theory of Literary Production*, 239).

28. Macherey argues (*A Theory of Literary Production*, 150) that "true analysis does not remain within its object, paraphrasing what has already been said; analysis confronts the silences, the denials and the resistance in the object—not that compliant implied discourse which offers itself to discovery, but that condition which makes the work possible, which precedes the work so absolutely that it cannot be found in the work." An obvious exception to my general point is *Tom Sawyer*, where the social fact of slavery is conspicu-

ously absent from the narrative itself. In all other instances advanced as evidence here, I find that the thing denied is in fact present, if somehow concealed, in the text. See Robinson, *In Bad Faith*, 113–14.

29. It appears, in fact, that Jameson is somewhat inconsistent in his characterization of the elements submerged in mass cultural texts. At one place in "Reification and Utopia" he argues that mass culture represses "fundamental social anxieties and concerns, hopes and blind spots, ideological antinomies and fantasies of disaster" by "the narrative construction of imaginary resolutions and by the projection of an optical illusion of social harmony" (141). Later in the same essay he describes the submerged content as "negative and critical of the social order" (144), and as offering "some sense of the ineradicable drive towards collectivity" (148). We must suppose that the utopian is here understood to include the ideal as it is implied in critical representations of its opposite.

30. Terry Eagleton, "Ideology, Fiction, Narrative," *Social Text* 2 (1979): 78.

31. Eagleton, *Criticism and Ideology* (London: Verso Editions, 1978), 69, 71.

32. Ibid., 74–75.

33. Ibid., 86.

34. Ibid., 87–88.

35. Ibid., 78.

36. Richard Dyer, "Entertainment and Utopia," in *Genre: The Musical*, ed. Rick Altman (London: Routledge & Kegan Paul, 1981), 184–85.

37. James Clifford, "On Ethnographic Self-Fashioning: Conrad and Malinowski," in *Reconstructing Individualism*, ed. Thomas C. Heller et al. (Stanford, Calif.: Stanford University Press, 1986), 147.

38. Peter L. Berger and Thomas Luckmann, *The Social Construction of Reality* (Garden City, N.Y.: Doubleday, 1966), 103.

39. Pierre Bourdieu, *Outline of a Theory of Practice*, trans. Richard Nice (London: Cambridge University Press, 1977), 19, 195, 188–89. In reading and rereading Bourdieu, I find much that anticipates and confirms my own thinking. His discussion of what he calls "the habitus" is especially stimulating. "It is because subjects do not, strictly speaking, know what they are doing that what they do has more meaning than they know. The habitus is the universalizing mediation which causes an individual agent's practices, without either explicit reason or signifying intent, to be none the less 'sensible' and 'reasonable'" (79).

40. Roy Wagner, *The Invention of Culture*, rev. ed. (Chicago: University of Chicago Press, 1981), 139, 141, 44–45, 59–60.

41. Geertz, "Ideology As a Cultural System," in *The Interpretation of Cultures*, 203–4, 218, 218 n. 41, 231.

42. Ibid., 218.

43. Geertz, "Conduct in Bali," 363.

44. Geertz, "Ideology As a Cultural System," in *The Interpretation of Cultures*, 219.

45. The denial of denial is necessary because that which is initially denied is actually true. The first denial may deceive others, but the second is requisite to the deception of the self. Herbert Fingarette elaborates on an identical "self-covering policy" in his *Self-Deception*, 48–49.

46. D. A. Miller, "Discipline in Different Voices: Bureaucracy, Police, Family, and *Bleak House*," Representations 1 (1983): 88 n. 21.

47. Greenblatt, "Invisible Bullets: Renaissance Authority and Its Subversion," *Glyph* 8 (1981): 41.

48. Greenblatt, "Shakespeare and the Exorcists," in *Shakespeare and the Question of Theory*, ed. Patricia Parker and Geoffrey Hartman (New York: Methuen, 1985), 164. Greenblatt develops his views on Marxism and poststructuralism in "Capitalist Culture and the Circulatory System," a chapter in *The Aims of Representation: Subject/Text/History*, ed. Murray Krieger (New York: Columbia University Press, 1987), 257–63.

49. Greenblatt, "Invisible Bullets," 47–48.

50. Ibid., 51. Greenblatt offers yet another perspective in his *Renaissance Self-Fashioning From More to Shakespeare* (Chicago: University of Chicago Press, 1980), 13: "But why should men submit to fantasies that will not nourish or sustain them? In part, More's answer is *power*, whose quintessential sign is the ability to impose one's fictions upon the world: the more outrageous the fiction, the more impressive the manifestation of power."

51. Ibid., 53.

52. Greenblatt makes this point in a number of different places, but perhaps most directly in *Shakespearean Negotiations: The Circulation of Social Energy in Renaissance England* (Berkeley and Los Angeles: University of California Press, 1988), vii: "Works of art, however intensely marked by the creative intelligence and private obsessions of individuals, are the products of collective negotiation and exchange." Cf. also *Shakespearean Negotiations*, 12; and "The Cultivation of Anxiety," 102.

53. Greenblatt, "Martial Law in the Land of Cockaigne," in *Shakespearean Negotiations*, 133–34, 135, 159.

54. Greenblatt, "Invisible Bullets," 51.

55. It should be obvious that this is not always the case. Popular American texts sometimes represent social and political authority as a threat to the interests of the assumed audience, and they sometimes represent the injustices of power without inviting their evasion. This overt, relatively unequivocal subversiveness is much more prevalent today than ever before in our history. In the wake of the civil rights movement, Vietnam, Watergate, and the advent of the new feminism, there is an increased audience readiness to acknowledge the injustices of the system and an expanding constituency of audience

members who regard themselves as un- or under-enfranchised, and thus more sinned against than sinning.

56. Mark Twain, *"Pudd'nhead Wilson"* and *"Those Extraordinary Twins,"* ed. Sidney E. Berger (New York: Norton, 1980), 19.

57. Hershel Parker, *Flawed Texts and Verbal Icons: Literary Authority in American Fiction* (Evanston, Ill.: Northwestern University Press, 1984), 132, 136. For a much fuller analysis of the bad faith of the composition, text, and reception of *Pudd'nhead Wilson*, see my essay, "The Sense of Disorder in *Pudd'nhead Wilson*."

INDEX

Althusser, Louis, 123–25

Bad faith, 112–14, 117–20, 123, 129, 136, 139, 143
Beard, James Franklin, 15, 20, 36
Berger, Peter L., 130–31
Bierce, Ambrose, 56–57, 77
Bloodworth, William, 8–9
Bourdieu, Pierre, 131

Cawelti, John, 53
Cleary, Michael, 105
Clifford, James, 130
Cooper, James Fenimore, 2, 14–20, 22–36, 38–39, 111, 113

Darwin, Charles, 46, 55
Davie, Donald, 27–30, 33
Davis, David Brion, 52
Dekker, George, 27
Doctorow, E. L., 107–9, 111
Donne, John, 69
Drinnon, Richard, 15–17
Dyer, Richard, 129–30

Eagleton, Terry, 125–27, 129
Erisman, Fred, 105

Fiedler, Leslie, 18, 27
Forrey, Robert, 56–57, 63
Franklin, Wayne, 22–23
Freud, Sigmund, 118–19

Gardiner, W. H., 32–34
Geertz, Clifford, 117–18, 132–34
Greenblatt, Stephen, 115, 137–40
Grey, Zane, 3–11, 111, 113

Haslam, Gerald, 105
Hawthorne, Nathaniel, 6
Hedrick, Joan D., 55, 57–58
Holland, Norman N., 118–20
Huckleberry Finn, Adventures of, 3, 52, 112–14, 116–17, 123, 126–29, 131–32, 134, 136

Jackson, Andrew, 13, 16, 20, 32, 35
Jameson, Fredric, 115–16, 120–22, 125
Jefferson, Thomas, 17
Jordan, David Starr, 58–59

Lambert, Neal, 53
Last of the Mohicans, The, 1, 14–39, 52, 111, 115–16, 119, 121, 127, 129, 132, 134, 141

INDEX

Leatherstocking Tales, 15, 18
London, Jack, 55–57, 72, 76–77, 111, 113
Luckmann, Thomas, 130–31

Macherey, Pierre, 124–25
Machiavelli, Niccolo, 138–39
Marx, Karl, 55, 135
McWilliams, John P., 18
Melville, Herman, 26–27
Miller, D. A., 135

Nietzsche, Friedrich, 55, 104, 130

Parker, Hershel, 143
Pearce, Roy Harvey, 18–19
Perry, John, 57
Philbrick, Thomas, 22–23
Pudd'nhead Wilson, The Tragedy of, 116, 121, 129, 141–43

Riders of the Purple Sage, 1, 3–10, 111, 116, 121, 129, 141
Rogin, Michael, 13–14, 16
Rossiter, Clinton, 105

Sand, George, 14–15, 18
Sartre, Jean-Paul, 118
Schaefer, Jack, 2, 79, 89, 105, 108, 111, 113, 136
Scharnhorst, Gary, 52
Sea Wolf, The, 1, 55–78, 111, 113, 116, 121–23, 128–29, 141

Shakespeare, William, 27, 35, 115, 138–41
Shane, 1–2, 79–109, 111, 113, 116–17, 119–23, 126–27, 129, 131, 134, 136, 140–41
Spencer, Herbert, 55
Starr, Kevin O., 77
Stasz, Clarice, 55, 57
Sterling, George, 56–57
Stowe, Harriet Beecher, 18
Swift, Jonathan, 104

Tom Sawyer, The Adventures of, 3, 112–14, 120, 122–23
Tompkins, Jane, 5, 22–23, 38
Turner, Frederick Jackson, 105
Twain, Mark, 3, 33, 111–14, 136, 143

Ude, Wayne, 4

Verne, Jules, 124
Virginian, The, 1, 8, 41–54, 111, 116, 119, 121–23, 128, 141

Wagner, Roy, 13
Walker, Franklin, 57
Ward, Susan, 55, 57
Washington, George, 25
Watson, Charles N., 56–57, 65, 73
Welcome to Hard Times, 107–9, 111
Whipple, T. K., 9
Wister, Owen, 5, 41, 53–54, 111

Yoder, Jon A., 56